Creative Embroidery

Dilys Blackburn

The Art of Crafts

First published in 1999 by
The Crowood Press Ltd
Ramsbury, Marlborough
Wiltshire SN8 2HR

British Library Cataloguing-in-Publication Data

A catalogue record for this book is available from the British Library.

ISBN 1 86126 252 3

Acknowledgements

Without the forbearance of my family I would not be able to achieve the time and effort
I give to this wonderful craft.
My main thanks go to all the members and friends of West Country Embroiderers, who
always work so hard and produce such wonderful creations.
My appreciation to my photographer, friend and neighbour Chris Robbins CPAGB. BPE2*
who has been so patient and helpful.

Typeface used: Melior © Adobe Systems Inc.

Designed and typeset by Annette Findlay
Printed and bound by Leo Paper Products, China

Contents

1 Introduction

I have been teaching creative embroidery for many years, and I particularly enjoy taking the beginner through the basic stitches and traditional techniques on to creative ways with fabric and thread. The course outlined here has been, and at the time of writing continues to be, very successful. I have used my own sample work throughout, together with that of the students. I encourage a 'one step at a time' approach, completing small samples and pieces of work, and keeping information and technical details to a minimum. In this way students make excellent progress and are eager to learn more.

I would strongly recommend that the beginner masters the basic skills covered in Chapters 1–10, completing the stitch samples and attempting most of the projects set out. All the information and illustrations shown provide the details required for steady progress in learning creative embroidery.

Chapters 11–14 include more advanced techniques involving both texture and colour. The keen amateur will find many stimulating ideas to try, and may like to adapt my suggestions and experiment further, mixing one technique with another.

Learning any art form can be very intense, and there are many embroidery classes or groups to join if you require help and guidance. Such groups have many other benefits, particularly as a source of ideas and encouragement, often through exhibitions. If you enjoy your embroidery, you could take the subject further and undertake a City & Guilds course or study a different aspect of the textile world.

Above all, I hope you receive great enjoyment from your achievements and choose to develop your knowledge and ability further after reading this book. In the meantime, welcome to the wonderful world of creative embroidery!

HISTORY

A visit to the Victoria and Albert Museum in London reveals all we need to know of our distant past, when the only sewing carried out was to make the clothes people wore or the rough stitched sacks they laid on. When improved fabric dyes were discovered, gradual changes started to appear. As trade between countries grew, ideas were interchanged and fashions and interior designs started to come alive.

Embroidery has always formed a part of worship, and through the ages designs seen on war banners and in heraldry represent various religious messages. Look at the Eastern countries with their colourful costumes depicting a way of life, designs which have been handed down through the ages and embroidered superbly using beautiful coloured threads. Today, the tribes of many countries are still decked out in their wonderful costumes and are a most intriguing subject to textile artists.

From the fifteenth century onwards, changes in fashion in the United Kingdom were great. Cloths covered with all-over patterns, house furnishings lavishly hung with canvas work, cushions, drapes, bed covers and large wall hangings – all these pieces were created by professional groups, who sometimes travelled the country. In the large country houses of the rich many pieces can still be seen today.

The introduction of the sewing machine left the craft of handwork far behind, and the designs for art and crafts went through a very drab period. During the eighteenth century many distinguished artists joined together to form the Arts and Crafts Movement, and a much-needed appraisal of the designs of the time took place, covering such disciplines as architecture, furniture, ceramics and textiles. These artists looked to nature for inspiration, using its subtle colours, movement and patterns, and designing beautiful items, which were long awaited and well received.

The sewing machine is once again taking a leading role in embroidery design, not only through free machining but also with the introduction of computerized machines which have introduced a new dimension for us to explore and enjoy. There are also many new materials and threads at our disposal. Metal, foam and rubber are amongst several being tried out by professional students and textile artists.

Professional English embroiderers not only carry out commissions but sell many pieces of their work all over the world. They also undertake lectures and teaching tours abroad, and thus take a leading role in the design and execution of creative embroidery.

Creative embroidery is progressing as never before, and it is hoped that despite all the new technology and materials at our disposal, the art of the needle does not disappear.

2 Basic Stitches

Stitches as we know them have been handed down from generation to generation, added to by other cultures, and even today we constantly experiment with them to create depth, texture and movement. Neat, regular stitching is so beautiful, and I refer to this as pure stitching. There is still a place for this today and it will appear regularly throughout this book. I have chosen to include only the stitches that are most often used; there are many books on stitches alone, but the regular embroiderer will find that many are only of limited use. If a certain design requires a stitch not included in this book, I will refer the reader to an appropriate text.

There are a great many different threads available, in beautiful, tantalizing colours – very delicate thin silks and very heavy ones, shiny and dull, twisted and slubbed, metallic and varigated in colour. Over time you will start to collect these wonderful yarns. If you are a beginner, start slowly and acquire those needed for each new piece of work, so that along the road of learning your collection will increase.

As a beginner you would be advised to obtain stranded cottons to start off with; these could be a single fine thread through to the full amount of six strands. Thicker, heavier threads would be used for more textured pieces of work as you progress.

The fabric on which you work depends on your subject and the technique that you are using. Your choice could be anything from very fine fabrics to the cottons, sheers and even heavier furnishing materials. For your first stitch sampler I would suggest that you work on cotton or poly-cotton. Refer to Chapter 8 for instructions on colourwashing your ground fabric with fabric paints.

The finished piece of work is so much more interesting and individual if you have considered a colour scheme. So often a well executed piece can look dull because of the lack of colour, so right from the very start of your work think – Colour, Texture and Movement.

Before commencing work you must prepare your embroidery ring by covering one of the rings with cotton tape. This helps to keep the fabric firm while you work. I would also advise that you work on double fabric, the top layer being your working ground fabric, the second layer your backing fabric. These two layers can be the same fabric top and bottom, and give a better tension of stitch, most advisable when stretching up a medium to large piece of work.

I strongly recommend that you keep a note book as you learn, as you will often want to keep a record of suggestions and ideas; it is to be encouraged that you make diagrams and even small drawings to help with such ideas.

STITCH-SAMPLER TIPS

◆ Cover an embroidery ring with cotton tape.
◆ Colourwash the top fabric.
◆ Work to a particular colour theme.
◆ Use different thicknesses of thread.
◆ Embroider through two layers of fabric.
◆ Think – Colour, Texture, Movement and Experiment!

FLAT STITCHES

Stem stitch

Always keep the thread to one side. Used for outlining and filling areas. Much thicker threads can be used for a heavier effect.

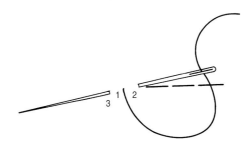

Back stitch.

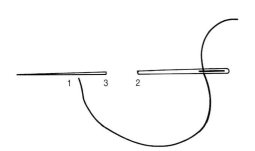

Stem stitch.

Running stitch

A nice free-flowing stitch, this stitch is placed very evenly, either close together or wide apart. Used to create darning patterns, it can be whipped by another thread. Creates flowing movement.

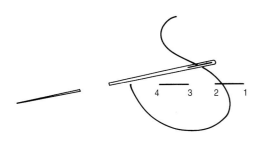

Running stitch.

Back stitch

Again, a very evenly placed stitch, used for outlining and movement, and to stitch other fabrics down, as in appliqué.

Fishbone stitch

Very effective for leaves and petals, this stitch can be closed or open. It can also form patterns.

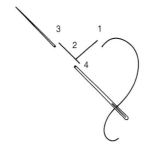

Fishbone stitch.

Long and short stitch

A stitch that creates shading with practice. The term 'long and short' is not always adhered to, particularly when filling large areas such as birds and animals. Can be carried out as if you were shading with a pencil. Never over-pack the area in question as the smooth effect will be lost.

Herringbone stitch

Herringbone and double running stitch are very similar. Used in the shadow work technique (*see* Chapter 6). A wonderful stitch of rhythm, it can follow shapes,

Long and short stitch.

Opposite:
Basic Materials: drawing pad, soft pencils, fabric marker pen, needles, scissors, tracing paper, collection of threads.

with stitches very close together or wide apart.

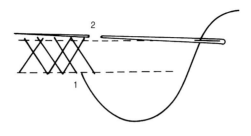

Herringbone stitch.

Seeding stitch

Very small straight stitches in every direction. Can be very effective for shading areas, filling in and blending colours.

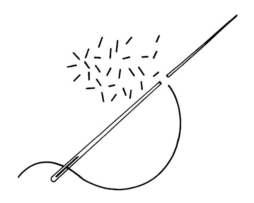

Seeding stitch.

Cross stitch

Carried out on canvas and counted thread work. When used freely in creative work the size of the stitch can be varied greatly, creating movement and shading.

The sampler shows the stitches listed, and also experimental stitches. You could experiment further with different thick-

nesses of thread, by laying stitches down in a pattern, or by laying one type of stitch over another.

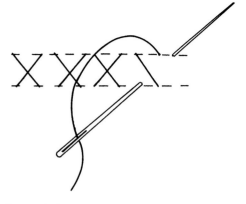

Cross stitch.

Flat stitch sampler (16sq cm).

LOOPED STITCHES

Buttonhole stitch

Used for edging and outlining, and for attaching other fabrics as in appliqué. Applied in circles it can form groups of flowers, or can be reversed, working outward with the stitch forming star-like flowers. Irregular buttonhole gives a lovely effect for petals, and different threads can be used for grasses and vegetation. It can also be used to cover loops, washers and other items.

Creton stitch

A free-flowing looped stitch that will fill areas, turn circles and create patterns and textures.

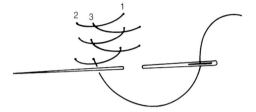

Creton stitch.

Fly stitch

Can be formal or free, filling areas, forming patterns and giving areas movement and shading.

The sampler shows the set stitches and also experimental stitches which have been moved to overlay each other or placed back to back. See how many different ways you can apply the stitches and what effects you can achieve. Experimentation will become a habit.

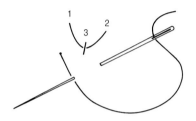

Fly stitch.

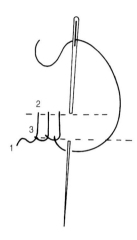

Buttonhole stitch.

Feather stitch

Similar to buttonhole but used in a lovely free-flowing motion representing plant growth.

Looped stitch sampler (16sq cm).

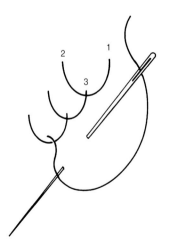

Feather stitch.

CHAIN AND KNOT STITCHES

Chain stitch

A very controlled, connecting looped stitch that can be as small as you can manage with a single thread, or much larger using a far thicker thread.

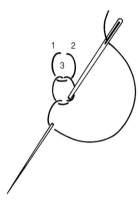

Chain stitch.

Open chain stitch

The same stitch as above, but opened wider. It can be carried out to produce a ladder effect and is very effective for heavy textures.

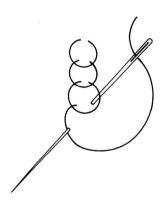

Open chain stitch.

Detached Chain Stitch

Worked separately, this version of the chain stitch is sometimes called 'lazy-daisy'. It will form flowers, leaves and is sometimes worked one over another.

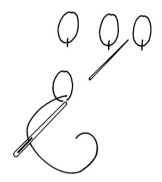

Detached chain stitch.

French knots

The secret of a successful knot is in the tension of the thread. A good tension will give a tight knot, leave off the tension completely and you will get a lovely loopy effect. This stitch creates areas that are ideal for the centres of flowers, or loose loops for undergrowth.

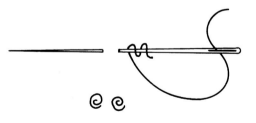

French knots.

Bullion knots

Take a back stitch and wind around the needle enough times to cover the length

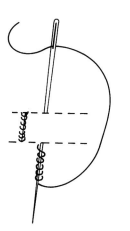

Bullion knots.

Chain and knot stitch sampler (16sq cm).

of the stitch. Controlling the tension, you then pull the needle through, creating a coil. With practice the stitch can represent perfect corn and barley.

The chain stitch and knot sampler shows the set stitches and also experimental work in movement and texture. Always be careful when applying French knots; apply them to give the effect of crunchy areas, rather than spotted about as if your work has measles.

COUCHING SAMPLER

This is a term given to the anchoring down of a laid thread on a surface using a different stitch. Start by making long stitches with the main thread, then with another needle and thread carry out the couching stitch. The main thread may move about to create your chosen design, the couching stitch must be chosen to translate the design effect you require.

The stitches used in the illustration below include brick couching (to resemble brickwork), straight stitch, fly stitch, herringbone, creton stitch, buttonhole, chain and plaited threads. Looped and couched slubbed yarn have also been used.

You can do a secret couching by using a fine thread of the same colour as the main thread, coming up and going down through the laid thread, thus hiding the couching stitch.

To complete this chapter, survey your samplers – do they all look colourful, exciting and show movement? By experimenting with the stitch and the thickness

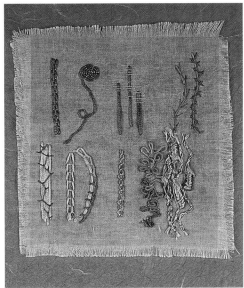

Couching stitch sampler (16sq cm).

of the thread, have you produced different effects to those illustrated? If so, you have learned from what you have seen and have experimented for yourself. Now follow Project 1 to demonstrate that at this stage you are capable of designing and working a piece of embroidery without help.

PROJECT 1

◆ Take a piece of calico or cotton, and using crayons or coloured pencils make a rubbing of tree bark.

◆ If this is impossible, draw your own illustration using coloured pencils or a '1H' pencil on the fabric.

◆ Prepare your ring with ground and backing fabric. Select your threads; think of your subject and alternate between thick and thin threads, with or without slub.

◆ Refer to your previous samplers and choose your stitches relative to the subject.

◆ You may wish to colourwash your fabric.

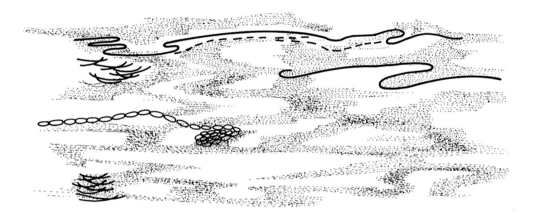

Tree bark drawing.

3 Pure Embroidery

By the term 'pure embroidery' I am referring to the execution of neat stitching for the sake of the stitch, without the interruption of added fabrics or other techniques. To complete a small piece of work, creating fine neat stitches to heavier work and making the stitch move about without losing its clarity, takes practice, but the finished effect is lovely.

In creative embroidery we never lack for design sources. We are surrounded by the most beautiful countryside, and everywhere we look there is colour and texture; ironwork, architecture, wood carvings, glass, ceramics and literature can also inspire. We never lack for ideas that can be translated into fabric and thread. We have all this to choose from but it can still prove difficult for the beginner. Too often a beginner will see a picture in a magazine or book that they would desperately like to try, but it is often far too adventurous to tackle at this stage.

My advice would be to turn to nature and wildlife books, birthday cards and gardening books, or to take a single spray of a flower, a leaf or some grass. Keep your design very simple to start with.

I have taken a single spray of a dog rose. Because the colours are a delicate pink and green, I have chosen to use a dupion furnishing fabric for the background material. The finished piece looks refreshing and natural and the needlework is clear and suits the whole design. A pale green colourwash on poly-cotton will also provide a natural background for such a subject.

It is good practice to draw the stitches you intend to use in the relevant spaces on paper to see if you are getting the desired effect.

TRANSFERRING THE DESIGN TO A FRAME

When you are satisfied with the subject that you are going to embroider, trace it from the book or magazine using soft tissue paper. Don't forget to keep it simple and do not clutter it up with other items. Transfer this tracing to your drawing pad and make the necessary notes regarding the stitches to be used. Put your colourwashed fabric and backing in the ring, place the tracing on top and secure it with

Detail of dog rose showing different stitches.

Design on tissue tacked out ready for work.

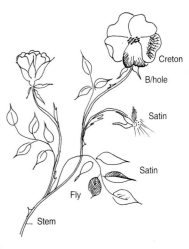

Dog rose – working drawing showing stitches.

pins. With a colour that you will not use in your embroidery, carefully carry out a running stitch all over the design as a guide. Be sure to finish off your cottons well because you are then able to carefully tear away and remove the paper. There may be an occasion when you need to trace your design on to your fabric, using a pencil. If so, always use a hard (1H) pencil. If you use a soft pencil, the lead may rub across your fabric and transfer on to your working threads. You now have your design ready to embroider. The tacking thread is carefully removed as you progress through the piece.

PROJECT 2

◆ Attach two layers of fabric to the frame or ring.
◆ You may wish to colourwash your ground fabric first.

Poppies by Heather Davenport (23cm x 36cm).

◆ Try out various stitches by drawing them in your drawing pad.
◆ Select or purchase your threads. Take care when choosing your colours – go for mellow harmonising tones and keep these threads apart from your stock.
◆ Tack your design as described above.
◆ Refer to your stitch samples for the appropriate stitches

Always refer to your reference picture or even the real flowers for the colour tones; be aware of the colour in the stems, the front and back of the leaves, and look how the veins in the petals give movement. Take notice of the formation and sometimes gentle colours of the centre. You must remember that you are an artist portraying your subject using textiles.

Having reached this point you will want to try something a little larger and more interesting.

PROJECT 3

◆ Trace one or two wild flowers with grasses.
◆ Assemble them in a pleasing and balanced design (*see* Chapter 10).
◆ Select your threads and beads.
◆ Colourwash your ground fabric if you wish.
◆ Prepare your frame with ground and backing fabric.
◆ Transfer your design.
◆ Embroider.

Keeping to the general idea of pure stitches and texture, let us now refer to books on birds. Choose a bird no bigger than a thrush, trace it and transfer this to your drawing pad. Then, again referring to your books, select the natural habitat for the particular bird that you are going to embroider. This time, instead of tracing the natural habitat, have a go at drawing it for yourself (a soft rubber might come in

Detail from *Woodbine* by Jackie Theobold.

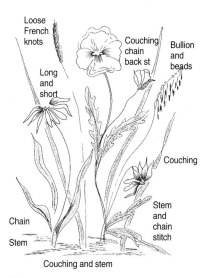

Wild flowers and grasses – working drawing showing stitches.

Opposite:
Dog Rose. Pure embroidery stitches using fine threads (10.5cm x 23cm).

Bird on apple blossom –
working drawing showing
stitches.

Dipper (15.5cm x 20.5cm).

useful at this point). This is a subject where you can really use your imagination on the various textures of undergrowth and tree bark.

PROJECT 4

◆ Colourwash your fabric.
◆ Prepare your frame with ground fabric and backing.
◆ Transfer your bird design to your frame or ring.
◆ Select your threads, beads, slubbed wools and so on.
◆ In your drawing pad try out various stitches and make a note of your ideas.

You will find long and short stitch, together with couching and fly stitch, are all you need to execute the bird. When using long and short stitch on the head and down the front of the bird, only use a single strand. Again, use some stitches for direction, filling in as you go. Do not over-pack your stitches or you may lose the smooth effect. If some of the ground fabric shows through, stand away from your work and you will see that it almost disappears.

You have now learned which stitch goes where and you are designing your own pieces of work and hopefully

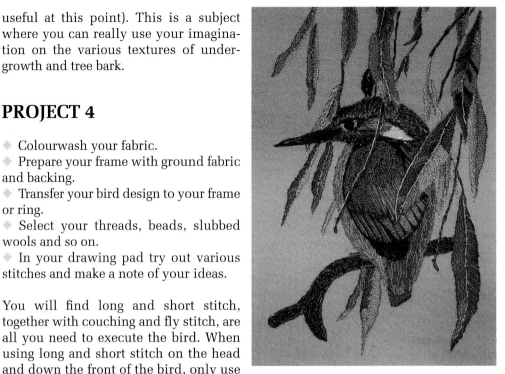

Detail of *Kingfishers*.

Wagtail.

Kingfishers by Heather
Davenport (45cm x 36cm).

embroidering interesting textures. You should always be thinking – Colour, Texture and Movement. Do not forget to experiment here and there, mixing different stitches together and introducing a few new threads.

Do not get too carried away; always learn to place your work at a distance and make sure that your textured areas are not

Girl on a swing by Liz Percival (15cm in diameter).

too weighty and that the colours are not becoming swamped. It takes some time to gain the experience to stop and declare a piece of work finished.

When you have finished one or two pieces of work you will want to frame them up, and this is covered in Chapter 10.

SUMMARY

Using birds and animals as subjects dates far back in time for the embroiderer. In Elizabethan times, wall hangings, caskets and mirror frames were very heavily worked with surface embroidery known as stump work. This is a very precise technique, which is still taught today, and involves padded people and animals, and compact surface embroidery of great intricacy. Padded people are dressed in needle weaving and look very realistic.

Birds and animals are still a popular subject for the embroiderer, and after you have completed one you may want to try a pair of birds or a larger single one, placing them in their own elaborate surroundings.

The same subject is covered in Chapter 11, introducing new techniques into the whole design, such as trapunto, adding fabrics that have been painted with fabric paint, and applying a much heavier approach to the surrounding area.

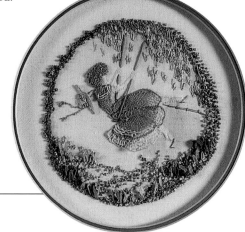

4 Jacobean Technique

'Jacobean' is a traditional technique of pure stitchery dating back to the seventeenth century. The design was reputed to have originated from the Orient, and 'the tree of life' growing from hillocks known as the terra firma. These trees had leaves, flowers and fruits of every kind, all very elaborate, incorporating insects and animals. The whole design was an extravaganza carried out with wools on twill weave fabric and was used for wall hangings, curtains and covers. Families would travel the country, employed by the country houses to carry out all of the refurbishing. When complete, which could take years, they would travel on to the next house and repeat the whole process. It was only the gentry that could afford such work, and these drapes, hangings and other work can still be seen today at famous country estates. Visit any National Trust properties and see how many types of embroidery you can spot.

We are going to use similar designs, but work them in finer threads and update the design, bearing in mind the delicate shadings used and the pretty infilling patterns that are so pleasurable to embroider. This is a pure stitching technique, working beautiful stitches for their own sake. A sense of satisfaction is guaranteed when you are able to do such neat work and when the end product is so pleasing.

The colours for each design are carefully chosen. Small amounts of sheer fabric are applied first and held down by back stitch, carefully cutting away the surplus. Then work the embroidery around the sheer. Any work on top of the sheer must be carried out last as the added work around the fine fabric will help to hold it down more firmly. If a pattern were stitched on to the sheer first, it may pull the fabric away from the back stitch.

Gold thread in the form of couching, chain stitch and herringbone, for example, are introduced very carefully. The gold thread is only used for an outline or for highlighting when necessary. You must not over-use the gold or the whole design may become a little brash.

When a large colour scheme is introduced, as in the tree of life, the whole piece appears to be far busier. A more subtle colour theme lends itself to the use of finer stitchery. Most of this work has been carried out on calico; this was a personal choice as I feel it looks clean and crisp and shows off the stitches more clearly.

Why not try to design your own piece? You could take the shape of an oak leaf and extend it, divide it up, create segments and add extra shapes to it. On your drawing pad try indicating where you would use a pattern or infilling, laying satin stitch then overlaying another thread on top. Always bear in mind that

70-year-old Jacobean cushion.

Opposite:
Detail from Jacobean cushion.

Tree of life sampler (20cm x 25cm).

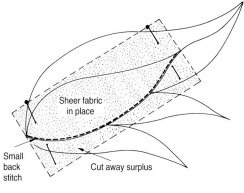

Adding sheer fabric to surface fabric – appliqué.

some areas need heavier stitching and some much lighter work. The weight distribution is of great importance. If your designs are too heavy on one side or heavy at the top and light at the bottom the whole design will appear out of balance.

Your choice of stitch and thickness of thread is crucial. Depending on the design, some stitches have to be graduated, working them to show off the movement within the shapes. You must always consider the shading of the colours too. If the design or the spaces within the design are small, a single thread is far more effective.

Leaf sampler.

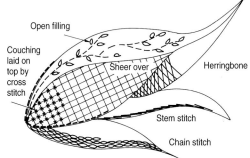

Detail of stitches.

Leaf sampler showing the use of coloured sheer fabric.

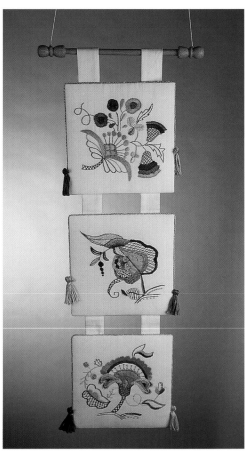

A three-drop hanging by Jose Lewis (each piece 13sq cm).

Waistcoat by Liz Taylor.

IDEAS

◆ Carry out as single pieces framed up.
◆ Present two or three pieces hanging from a rod.
◆ Divide a cushion cover into four sections, with one design in each section.
◆ Create lovely designs for waistcoats or pockets.
◆ Use colour themes to depict the seasons.

PROJECT 5

◆ Draw your Jacobean design on paper.
◆ Using a light box or by attaching the pieces to a window, copy the design on to calico using a '1H' pencil.
◆ Apply the design and backing fabric to a ring or frame (the backing fabric could be cotton).
◆ Select a colour theme and choose stranded cottons, fine threads and a gold sewing thread.
◆ Select a sheer that you can see the design through, if required.
◆ Do not forget to shade your colours from light to dark.
◆ Introduce very small beads to the design, if desired.

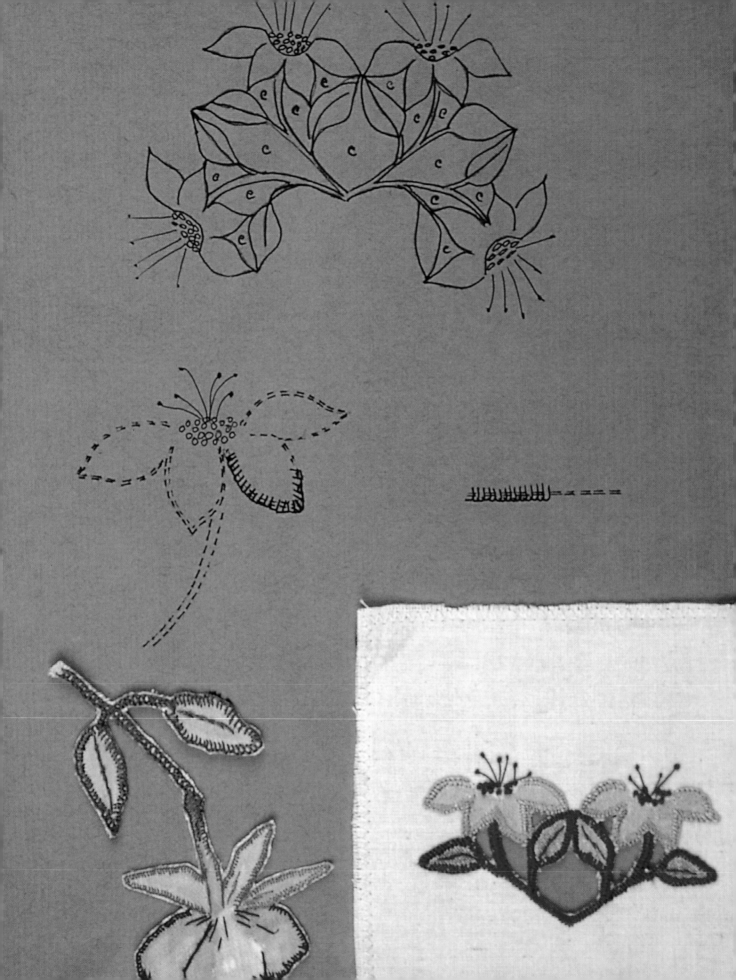

5 Cut Work

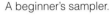

In this chapter I am going to cover the technique of cut work in its most simple form. There are other forms of cut work that come under the heading of 'Broderie Anglaise', otherwise known as Madiera work, Renaissance, Richelieu or Reticella. Basic cut work is more straightforward and can be integrated into our creative embroidery. The other forms mentioned are very ornate, with more cut spaces, bars and infillings, and are altogether more elaborate. The traditional techniques were worked with white thread on firm white linen; today we can push the boundaries with colour and fabrics, but we must always remember that the piece worked must be suitable for its purpose.

DESIGN

A lot of thought must be given to the design or the whole piece of work will go awry. Use a formalized flower shape and leaves, which must be placed so that the points of the leaves and the petal shapes meet. This will give well-shaped spaces which can be completely embroidered around. The extra fabric can now be cut away with care.

At the beginning of the chapter is a simple design which was created by tracing one small spray of flowers, turning it round and tracing it to form a repeat pattern.

METHOD

Carry out your first attempt on medium weight calico or firm linen. Transfer your design to the fabric using a light box or the window method. Lay your fabric over the design and trace it using a pointed '1H' pencil or watercolour pencil (the same colour as your threads). Go over the design with a single thread with two rows of close running stitch. This is used as a guide and strengthener for the buttonhole stitch, which is applied to the whole of the design. The cord edge of the buttonhole must be kept to the edge that is going to be cut away. You can cut away from

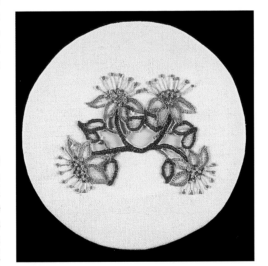

A beginner's sampler.

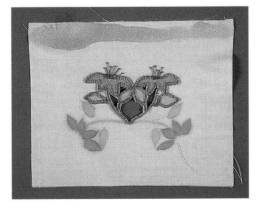

A beginner's sampler which has been fabric painted.

Opposite:
Cut work design sheet.

Cut free sampler.

both sides of the fabric, but I prefer to do it from the right side, keeping as close to the edge as possible.

Again, this is a pure embroidery technique carried out very neatly with great precision, and is a lovely technique.

You can, if careful, stitch a small spray of flowers and then cut it completely free so that it can be added to other work. I would advise the application of iron-on vilene to the back of the fabric first.

IDEAS

Use cut work as:

◆ a small design for a birthday or special card

◆ table or place mats
◆ a cushion
◆ a fashion item on blouses, pockets and cuffs
◆ a design for a picture with coloured silk behind the embroidery.

PROJECT 6

◆ Using my design, or better still a design of your own, apply the design to the fabric using a light box or the window method.
◆ Using a firm calico or linen, choose a colour theme and complete the piece, as described.

6 Shadow Work

This is one of the most delicate forms of embroidery, working on the finest sheer fabric with very fine threads. A popular technique in the eighteenth century, considered to have originated in India, it was always worked on very fine organdi. Again, this is a form of pure embroidery, using very fine and precise stitchery. Although you should be proficient with your stitching before you attempt this technique, I have found that with careful instructions, beginners have carried out some very pleasing work, and are very taken by its delicacy.

A free-flowing flower design will show off this technique to its best. Draw your design on paper, then use a light box or the window method to secure your fabric over the design. Using a sharp pointed coloured pencil the same colour as your thread, trace the design. Because you are using such a fine silk organdi or nylon chiffon fabric, it is most important that one of your embroidery rings has been covered with tape. This not only keeps the fabric taut, but it protects the material from giving way at the edge of the ring. Use fine threads and a fine crewel needle; if you choose a thicker thread use a thicker needle, but the finer work looks much clearer. The main stitch is herringbone, which creates two parallel lines on the surface, the pattern of the stitch laying at the back, thus creating the shadow. Other stitches incorporated are back and running stitch, chain stitch and buttonhole eyelets. French knots may be used if desired, but do take care as they can disappear to the rear if you use the same hole.

Before you start, knot your thread and take two very small stitches on the spot, holding the knot away from the fabric a little. Carry out your embroidery, cutting off the knot when you have finished.

In my butterfly design, the stitches are herringbone, back stitch and eyelets, and the feelers are finished with French knots. You may wish to try a coloured design on white sheer, depicting flowers and leaves in their true colours. Take care that you are not too heavy with colour or thickness of threads, or the work may become too hard-looking and the delicate technique will be spoilt.

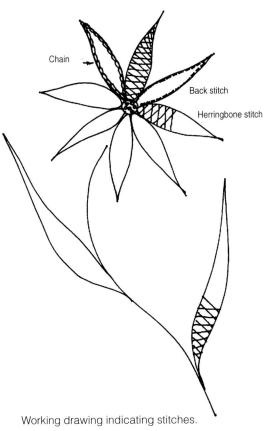

Chain

Back stitch

Herringbone stitch

Working drawing indicating stitches.

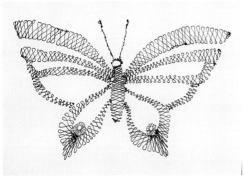

Butterfly.

Shadow appliqué butterfly.

SHADOW APPLIQUÉ

This is a form of shadow work using another layer of fabric at the back, thus creating a deeper shadow. Pin small pieces of coloured sheer to the back of the piece, then carry out your embroidery. You must make sure that the very close back stitches attaching the fabrics are well executed; they must make a continuous line round the design. Then, using sharp scissors, carefully cut away the surplus fabric.

An alternative would be to use a coloured sheer on which to work the design, adding another layer of the fabric to the back. As you can see from the insect design, it is a very attractive form of shadow appliqué.

The permutations can be very interesting – blue on blue, or pink on pink. You could also mix your colours, thus creating different attractive shadings.

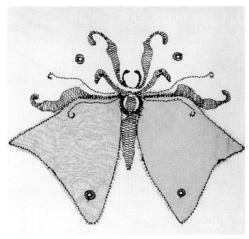

Insect - green on green.

SHADOW QUILTING

This technique uses coloured shapes of fabric between two layers of sheer, using back stitches around the shapes to trap them in position and form your design.

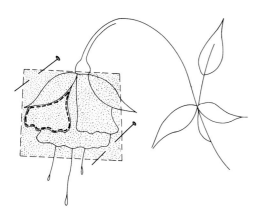

Working drawing indicating stitches. Applying sheer fabric to rear - shadow appliqué.

Opposite:
Pure shadow work - white on white.

31

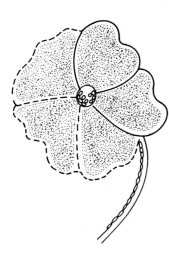

Shadow quilting.

This type of work can look quite harsh and is sometimes softened with a little fine surface stitching.

SHADOW ITALIAN QUILTING

In this technique you use two layers of sheer fabric, and the design is of a lineal type using back stitches to create fine channels through which a coloured wool or thicker thread is threaded from the back.

There are many more interesting ways of using this beautiful technique, which do require some experimentation. I have covered this in more advanced form in Chapter 14.

IDEAS

Use shadow work:

- as a birthday or special occasion card
- to create a design which is laid over coloured fabric and framed up
- to make up a cushion cover colour co-ordinated to your furnishings
- as a border for a bathroom curtain
- in fashion and bridalwear.

PROJECT 7

Creating a card for a special occasion.

- Design a favourite flower.
- Frame up a piece of white sheer and draw the design on to it.
- Using the colours of the flower, execute the embroidery.
- Take a card (these can be purchased from an art shop) and apply a piece of coloured fabric to the inset.
- Apply the piece of embroidery over the top, attaching it with adhesive.
- Attach it one side at a time to avoid ripples.

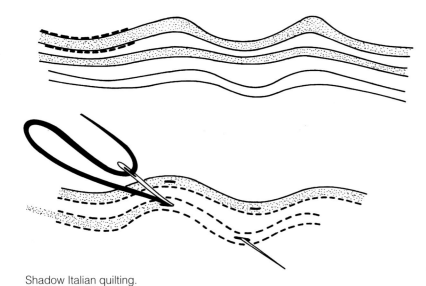

Shadow Italian quilting.

7 Quilting

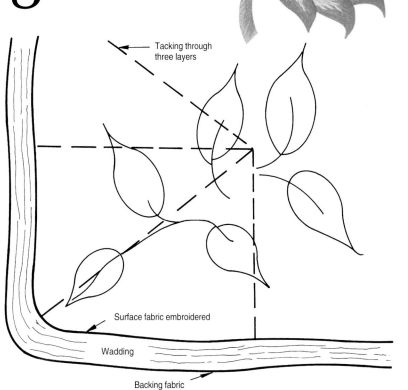

Quilting was probably invented to provide warm clothing and padding under armoury. It consists of three layers of fabric stitched together in a regular form, creating a grid or pattern. As time progressed these patterns became very ornate and elaborate and in the seventeenth century decorative waistcoats, jackets and skirts were the height of fashion. The craft of quilting was kept alive in the north of England and Wales, where ladies would make their own quilts using traditional patterns. When the English landed in the Americas they took the technique with them and it became an important part of life. During the past fifteen years or so great advancements have been made, not only with the designs, but there are now many more coloured fabrics available. The cutting and piecing together of these lush colours has promoted a new interest in the technique throughout England and America. Although they are embroidery techniques, quilting and patchwork are today taught as separate subjects.

Labels on diagram: Tacking through three layers / Surface fabric embroidered / Wadding / Backing fabric

appear. Remove the tacking and make up the finished work.

Embroidery prepared for English quilting.

ENGLISH QUILTING

This style of quilting consists of an all-over raised effect worked through three layers of fabric – the surface fabric, the wadding and then the backing fabric. If you are embroidering a piece of work that you also wish to quilt, complete the embroidery first then assemble the three pieces of fabric together, tacking them out into the grid so that they do not move. Carry out the quilting using a back or running stitch, taking care not to pull too tightly as you do not want puckering to

ITALIAN QUILTING

This technique is used when you require a raised line to the fabric; it is useful for the stems of flowers, lineal and pattern designs or for movement. To make the line show up well use a strong backing fabric such as calico or strong cotton. Work two parallel lines of stitching through the two fabrics, then thread through these lines with a long needle, working from the rear using cord or similar thread depending on the design. The same method is used for shadow Italian quilting.

TRAPUNTO QUILTING

A technique used for raising certain parts of the design. Work a very small back stitch through the surface and backing fabrics to the shape or area required to be raised, make a small cut to the backing fabric only and stuff the area with wadding a little at a time. Stitch over the slit to strengthen it. Depending on your design, you may choose to embroider over these padded areas, but do be careful with the tension of your stitching if the stitches are too tight they will pull down the padding and the effect will be lost. This is a very useful technique for padding out petals, leaves, animals, birds and people.

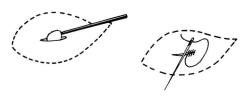

Trapunto quilting.

APPLIQUÉD TRAPUNTO

Carry out trapunto as instructed, but first apply a piece of fabric to the surface with back stitch in the chosen shape. Lay the fabric with the grain, carry out the back stitch and stuff the shape from the rear. The applied fabric could either be left with a rough edge or trimmed away; in very textured work a frayed edge works very well, but you must take care not to fray too far back.

The technique of English quilting is an art form, and the use of the fabrics, threads, plus the preparation of the layers is very precise. When quilting is added to creative embroidery it is dealt with in a

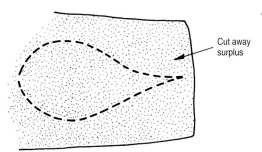

Appliquéd trapunto.

Cut away surplus

more casual way, but care must be taken so the layers do not move and puckering does not appear. Quilting is used to highlight areas or throw back some areas, creating a shadow effect.

In more advanced embroidery, many different techniques are mixed together for the benefit of the design.

IDEAS

Embroider and quilt:

- a cushion or waistcoat
- a wallhanging
- bags and purses.

PROJECT 8

To create a cushion.

- Prepare your design on tissue paper.
- Transfer the design to the top fabric only, then place the ground fabric and muslin into an embroidery frame or ring.
- Carry out the embroidery.
- Remove the piece from the frame.
- Prepare your three layers, tacking them out.
- Carry out your quilting (by hand or, if careful, by machine – *see* Chapter 14).

Opposite:
Cushion fabric painted on calico with English quilting.

8 Painting Fabric

Any type of fabric, whether natural or synthetic, can be painted, but smooth fabrics are the best. Similarly, most fabric paints on the market are satisfactory, but I prefer the thicker type as it is easier to control. All paints will dilute with water, and the wetter you make the fabric the more the paint will penetrate the fibres; thicker paint will remain on the surface. It is advisable to wash and iron your fabric first, and this is imperative when using calico as the dressing in this material differs immensely and can affect the finished colours. When all your painting has been completed, the fabric must be dried and ironed to make it colourfast. Protect your ironing board and fabric with paper, both underneath and on top of the fabric. There are specialized silk paints, however painting on silk is an entire subject on its own and is not covered in this book, although silk paints can be used on many fabrics. They can also be added to other fabric paints to achieve colour tones and I have found these to be successful. For detailed advice on how to paint on silk, see *Silk Painting* by Jenni Milne, also in the Crowood 'Art of Crafts' series.

Fabric painting should be seen as fun; most people get very uptight at the prospect, but it really is not as hard as you think. Just remember that there are no set rules to follow, it is only by having a go that you will learn how to mix your colours and the amount to apply to the fabric.

COLOURWASHES

Take the right amount of fabric, allowing extra material for framing up. Put the ground fabric into the ring or embroidery frame; it is far easier to apply paint to the fabric when it is taut. Lightly dampen your fabric with a water spray as this helps the paint to float and merge on the material. Mix your colour, testing it out on the material to ensure it is the right strength. If you want a lighter shade, use more water.

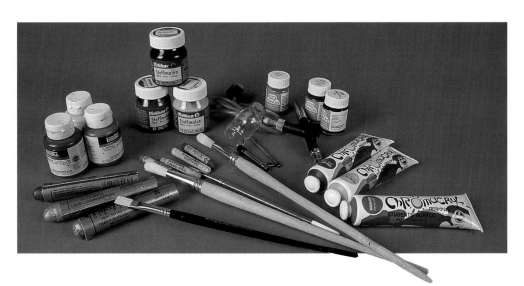

Materials for fabric painting: primary colours in fabric paints, transfer paints, acrylic paints, selection of brushes, artist paint sticks.

Opposite:
Poppy sampler colourwashed with fabric paint then painted with acrylics, applied embroidery.

To achieve a green colourwash for an all-over background, put some yellow and blue paint on the side of your mixing plate with a little water in the middle. Start by adding some yellow to the middle of the plate followed by a little blue for a lighter shade of green. Apply this colour to the top of your fabric using a large brush, adding a little more blue all the time so that the green colourwash becomes deeper in tone towards the bottom of the fabric. This will give you a very natural background of different shadings. Dry and iron your fabric.

Fabric painting takes time and a little practice, and you may experience a few failures, but if the piece is still wet and un-ironed, you can wash it and have another attempt. If you find the piece is too pale once you have dried and ironed it, go through the procedure again, giving it another coat. You must remember to wet the fabric all over with the colourwash or you will be left with watermarks.

A mouth diffuser

This is a very small instrument obtained from art suppliers. It creates a sprayed effect on the fabric, achieved by blowing down a metal tube suspended in a pot of colour. It takes a lot of practice and is punishing on the muscles of the mouth.

Spray gun

This is an expensive method, as a small compressor is also required. It does, however, produce a lovely even application of paint to fabric, and you can also apply one colour over another. It is particularly successful when used on stencils. The gun is a delicate instrument and it can get clogged up from time to time, so it takes a lot of practice to use the tool and achieve the correct consistency. The gun has to be very clean to work well, but the effect it produces is very worthwhile.

APPLYING PAINTS

Another easy method of applying paints is to mix your colour and to sponge it very lightly on to damp fabric. This is a way of merging two or three background colours together and can create a very interesting effect. After drying and ironing such a background you could make a potato print of a leaf or flower, and print a design straight on to the fabric using a stronger paint.

Take some leaves from your garden, the back of the leaf is better for printing, apply a thick paint to the leaf and print on the fabric, pressing carefully all over. You can obtain lovely prints and create a free-flowing design to complement different embroidery techniques.

There are many other ways of applying paint to fabric, using different tools and equipment.

Daisies. The background has been sprayed with fabric paint and the flowers painted in acrylics.

Stencils

This is probably one of the easiest forms of printing on fabric. Most art shops sell ready-made stencils, or you can design your own and cut them from mounting card with a card knife. You can also obtain a waxed stencil paper. Secure your stencil in position with masking tape then apply your colour quite firmly using a stencil brush. If your paint is too watery you will find that it will run and you will not obtain a clear cut stencil line. You can play around with your design by applying one print over another using different colours, or using a sponge in place of a brush which gives a mottled, softer effect. Do not forget to wipe clean your stencils if you are using them more than once. Try colourwashing the fabric first then using your stencil prints. This method is ideal for repeat patterns or motifs.

Transfer paints

These paints should only be applied to synthetic fabrics, but I have found that mixed fabrics also receive them quite well. You must mix and test the colours before applying them to the material, as you will see that the colours do change once applied.

Draw your design on to cartridge paper then paint it in. Do not leave any blobs of paint, painting as quickly as possible using continuous strokes so that it is applied very evenly. When the paint is dry, place the design on top of your fabric and place another piece of paper over that. Using your iron at the required heat for the material, iron over the design; do not allow the papers to move or the finished design will be blurred. The longer you iron, the darker the print will be, so keep taking a look so that you get the depth of colour that you require. You can use the design two or three

Cotton colourwashed then stencilled using fabric paints.

Sampler, painted then quilted.

Beginner's sampler, painted then quilted.

times, however the print will be paler each time.

You must remember that turning your design over will mean that it appears on your fabric in reverse. Transfer paints are well worth experimenting with, as you can achieve such gentle colour tones, and can move your design about to create an all-over design.

Transfer crayons

The instructions for transfer paints also apply to transfer crayons. Having drawn up a design, apply your crayons evenly, trying not to leave flakes of wax on the paper as they will create smudges and spoil the whole idea. The paper is then turned on to the fabric as instructed.

Acrylic paints

Watered down acrylic paints will provide a colourwash background. If a thicker consistency of paint is used to paint a design on to the surface of the fabric, you will find that the fabric is on the stiff side and the embroidery is a little harder to carry out. I use these paints very carefully when I wish to paint a design, usually flowers or grasses, that can then be complemented by embroidery.

SUMMARY

Most techniques of applying paint take practice, and perhaps those of you who are new to this craft will want to try them out at a later date. When you have gone further with your embroidery it is hoped that you will attempt one or two of these painting techniques to give further depth and interest to your work.

One thing all of us must remember is that painting on fabric is a means of portraying and accentuating each design, and must not be used as a design in itself. A happy balance must be obtained between the painting, the embroidery and any other technique included in the finished work. We consider ourselves textile artists, not solely painters or collage artists; each technique must complement the other.

Poppy sampler colourwashed with fabric paint then painted with acrylics.

9 Texture and Manipulation

This area of embroidery is very exciting, concentrating on experimentation with various types of fabrics, threads and anything else you wish to include to achieve the desired finished effect. The world around us is full of different textures and ideas, and without texture the work would look flat, dull and uninteresting. The word 'texture' covers many different traditional techniques – cut work, white work, hardhanger, pulled and drawn work, smocking, quilting, stump work and appliqué. These are all techniques that change the surface of the working fabric, creating spaces, depth of colour and manipulation. When you venture into the realms of texture, whatever its form, you become aware that you are working in another dimension, creating light and dark areas and movement through the use of textured threads and the density of the stitching.

Manipulation covers a multitude of alterations to the texture of the fabric such as:

- fraying
- rouching
- pleating
- weaving
- tucking
- rolling
- gathering
- padding
- burning
- cutting.

The key word here is experiment. It is only by observation, trial and error that you will become more experienced in the adaptability of fabric and thread. When applying pieces of fabric to the ground fabric as in appliqué, the grain of both fabrics should lay in the same direction to prevent distortion; in creative embroidery and when working with textures, this does not necessarily apply.

You will start to collect all sorts of fabrics in many different colour tones, and should get into the habit of keeping every little piece no matter how small. I collect all my bits and pieces in separate colour-coded boxes. The best tip I can give you is to have a box of white and cream fabrics of all types, from sheer and lacy to thick and textual. It takes a long time

Detail of texture and manipulation.

to accumulate a good variety, which can be coloured as and when required for each project.

PROJECT 9

To create a coloured textured sampler.

◆ Colourwash your ground fabric.
◆ At the same time, colourwash small pieces of other fabrics together with some threads.
◆ Place the ground fabric and backing fabric in your ring or frame.
◆ Apply fabrics and threads creating and experimenting with as many different textures as possible.

The green sampler was worked on poly-cotton using many different types of fabrics, all colourwashed with fabric paint first. I have included card pieces, trapunto padding, some padded pebble shapes, tucking and rouching, folding and fraying, small strips of fabric rolled up to form small coils, pieces of fabric applied one over another, circles cut out, quartered and stitched down, and leaf shapes frayed and sewn on.

If you wanted to take this technique further, turn to calico and carry out a formal sampler. Work on a background of approximately 30sq cm, divide it into equal squares and place a different texture in each square. Although this is a sampler it can look very attractive, particularly if framed up using rouched strips.

For 'The Beach' project (p. 45) there is no need to use a set design as you can work from your imagination. This subject gives you more scope to try out and experiment with texture – pebbles in padding and satin stitch, shells flat and raised, bits of wood and cord, metal washers covered with buttonhole stitch, running stitches to represent ripples on the sand, seeding and tiny beads for gritty areas and stitches for grasses and other vegetation.

Calico sampler by Liz Percival.

Detail of calico sampler.

Opposite:
Sampler – texture and
manipulation.

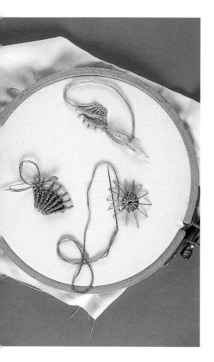

Needle-weaving sampler.

It is not difficult to achieve this shell effect. Cut a piece of felt or pelmet vilene to the shape you require. Then lay stitches over the top to create a grid on which to weave. Starting at the top and to one side, take your needle under two stitches, then go back over the last one and under the next one in one movement. In this way you are covering each grid stitch in a weaving motion. You can also sew down a large holed bead, repeating the same process. You can, however, work this type of weaving directly flat on the fabric. Try many different ways as it is an attractive technique. Let your imagination run free!

Above:
Beach textures by Dorothy Bennett (20cm in diameter).

Left:
Beach textures by Jackie Theobold (20cm in diameter).

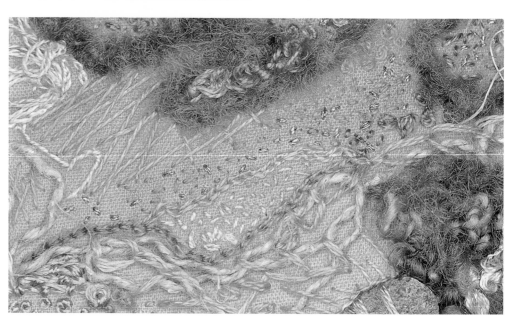

Beach textures in detail by Jackie Theobold.

PROJECT 10

'The Beach'

◆ Colourwash the fabric in a shade to suit the subject.
◆ Place the ground and backing fabrics in an embroidery frame or ring.
◆ Select different threads and beads.
◆ Carry out your own interpretation of a small section of beach.

SUMMARY

Experimenting with fabrics and threads not only adds a further dimension to embroidery, but it makes us more aware of the capabilities of fabric. It enables us to translate what we see using textiles.

Today many different commodities are used, including glues, rubber and foam, glass, metal and wood. We burn and distress fabric, and try all manner of things to convey our thoughts and ideas using the medium of art. Some experiments may not work, but this should not prevent us from trying other ideas and pursuing certain thoughts to obtain a result. Traditional techniques were carried out to set ideas using particular fabrics and threads; today there are no rules and techniques are mixed with one another, 'experiment' being the key word. However, playing with techniques and adding objects to our work is for the purpose of translation of design. We must not forget that we are dealing with fabric and stitch, and the finished work must reflect this.

10 Design and Presentation

Many people feel that drawing and design is difficult, yet this is not so. You will need to practise and you may need some advice and general tips, but it forms an integral part of the embroidery process. This chapter looks at various design ideas.

You must begin with the correct tools – pencils '4 to 6B' and '1H', charcoal and a selection of coloured pencils, a soft rubber, drawing pad or paper, tracing paper and pencil fixative spray, essential over charcoal and other heavy drawings before tracings are taken. Have one or two reference books on the countryside, animals, birds and wild flowers.

LEAVES

Collect some leaves from your garden. Study them in detail, including front and back, the change in colour, the veining and patterning. Lay them on paper and draw round them, or try and draw a page of leaf designs free-hand. You can lay them on paper and have them photocopied, use your coloured pencils and add shading, and use your '1H' pencil to add the vein detail. At this point you could try indicating some stitches.

You could even draw a spray of leaves, or alternatively arrange several leaves on a piece of paper and photocopy them. A lot can be achieved with the photocopier – the print can be made paler or much darker, enlarged or reduced.

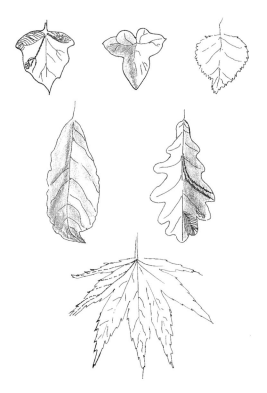

Leaves.

FLOWERS

Select a flower from a book and trace it, then transfer this tracing on to paper. You can trace different flowers, enlarging your design as you go; by placing several together in a natural way, you can create designs to transfer to fabric as described in Chapter 3. Once you have attempted this method of design, try drawing the flowers free-hand with a soft pencil. Alternatively, you could photocopy the flower, and could progress to making

Opposite:
Pattern on a theme – shells and sea.

Rearrangement of
photocopy.

FISH

Using a reference book, trace and draw a
fish, compiling a design by introducing
waterweed, stones and shells. This is a
very good subject for including subtle
colour changes and textures. You may
also be able to introduce some coloured
sheers by laying them on the ground fabric, giving a watery effect, and embroidering on top. There is great scope for
experimentation in your work.

TREES

I have outlined a few suggestions of basic
tree formations. A good way to convey
these ideas to paper is to use a '6B' pencil or better still charcoal. Take a large
piece of lining paper, break off a piece of
charcoal, medium thickness. Drawing
with the side of the charcoal, go from the
roots up the tree and release the pressure
out over the branches. You can get lovely
movement and almost bring the tree to
life. Take time to practise this technique.
I hope you find it enjoyable, but you will
get rather dirty. When satisfied with your

three or four photocopies of one spray,
cutting them all out and rearranging them
to create a new design.

Trees drawn using charcoal.

drawing, spray it with a fixative. Photo-copy the designs to make them smaller or larger. You will find they can be utilized in many ways, from quilting to appliqué, pure embroidery to heavy textures.

The roots of a tree are a design in them-selves, with lumps, growths, fungi and mosses. You couldn't wish for anything better through which to experiment with your embroidery techniques.

There are many subjects that can be developed from architecture, wrought iron work, landscapes, brick and stone work. You can collect ideas from maga-zines and cards, photocopy them, cut them up and arrange a design. Don't think about embroidery when you draw. Draw for the sake of drawing; it does not have to be perfect and is for guidance only. If you persevere you can not only find it extremely helpful but most rewarding. When you are able to draw your own design, have it photocopied and apply some colour, then pin it up at a distance and live with it for a day or two to ensure that you are happy with the design. Many embroiderers tend to choose a specific subject for their designs with a negative or abstract background to highlight the subject. Totally abstract work is less popular, however some abstract ideas can be quite exciting and thought provoking.

PATTERN

Firstly, let us refer to the use of basic stitches to form a pattern. Even a line of a repeat stitch forms a repeat pattern. Work buttonhole in blocks, back to back or interlocked, using alternate colours or dif-ferent threads. Try using other stitches, for example fly stitch, satin stitch, creton stitch and herringbone. Chain stitches can make a travelling pattern or coiled circles. A good all-over pattern could be used on its own, or you could use a geometric design as a border pattern or as a sur-round to a panel.

Pattern in stitches.

CIRCLES

Experiment with creating circle shapes, as shown, to see what you can come up with. I have tried some free drawn circles, in blocks, in strips, some shaded, some outlined, introducing semi-circles or overlaid. Just playing about with shapes can produce some interesting designs and ideas.

Tree root.

Patterns using circles.

SQUARES

The square can become an oblong, squares can appear inside other squares or can interrupt and overlay each other. You could have a very well-balanced design and then fill the shapes with stitches as a stitch sampler, with a pattern border around the whole design. Try testing various patterns for yourself, perhaps including themes such as leaves, fish or shells.

I have used a 15cm square and divided it into well-balanced sections. I have then introduced shapes as a repeat pattern to fill the sections. Remove the section lines from your drawing, and review what you have drawn, fitting in any repeat pattern ideas. Transfer your design to your fabric, thinking of the colours, stitches and techniques you can use. I have completed my piece by mounting it on card then re-mounting it on card covered with hand-made paper (*see* p. 46).

Pattern using squares as a grid.

BUILDINGS

Architecture was the inspiration for the design used in this pattern. The design is basically an archway divided into sections, the sections repeating the arch. Each arch is filled with a pattern representing the sky and the earth. Depending on its size, this type of pattern could be translated in a variety of different ways, such as pure stitching, cut work, or by laying layers of bright colours over each other and stitching to create spaces which can be cut back to reveal certain colours, a technique called reverse applique.

COMPOSITION

Some people have a natural ability for achieving a well-balanced composition, whilst others find it difficult. It may take a photographer years to learn the art of a good photograph taken in seconds. An artist, particularly a watercolour artist, takes years to perfect that spontaneous landscape. The art is in the looking, for both depth and balance. A photographer, for example, would not consider a landscape with an electric pylon in the middle, and would not take a picture when the distant hills met right in the middle of the piece. The art is in selecting the view and standing in the correct spot.

So far I have dealt with the composition of flowers, leaves, birds and so on, working with threads and textures on light to dark backgrounds, however the

Pattern using archways.

Pattern on a thistle theme.

overall balance must always be considered. There is a simple rule you can follow – take the total size of your design and divide it into thirds, the bottom third being the heaviest in content and embroidery, the middle third being of a medium weight in content and work and the top third being the lightest. This technique can be seen in the line drawing of wild flowers and grasses on page 17, and also applies to pictures and wall-hangings.

Soft furnishings work slightly differently, depending on the techniques used and the purpose of the piece. The correct balance for cushions, for example, would be two thirds worked, one third plain. You could, of course, use an all-over design or pattern, taking the technique, depth of colour and tone into account. The final effect should be well-balanced and pleasing to the eye.

Remember that it is an acquired skill and that the preparation of a working plan together with some suggested stitches and textured samples are necessary to highlight any faults and achieve the desired result. Your intended colour depths and the tonal values you propose to use should all balance out.

As I have said, your drawings do not have to be perfect. If you are indicating plants and trees, you are not expected to do so in detail. Record what you see, and write down as many notes and ideas as you wish, regarding colour, stitch and texture. It is very unusual for an embroiderer to sew without some form of design or investigation of one's subject.

You may be a true beginner at drawing, but please do keep trying. Do not forget it is your drawing and your plan of work, it need not be for anyone else's eyes and no-one else need understand it.

It is a good rule to keep your sketches and ideas in a folder, as you may wish to refer to them in the future. Some ideas may require you to carry out small samplers and trials, and these should also be kept for reference.

IDEAS

Take a flower or a leaf and enlarge the image using a photocopier. Turn it around to create a four-way pattern, ideal as a design for a panel or cushion. Repeat the idea using a lineal design or create patterns from feathers, butterfly wings, shells, fish, flowers or leaves.

PROJECT 11

To create a charcoal drawing of a tree.

◆ Trace the design.
◆ Colourwash your fabric.
◆ Place the ground and backing fabric in an embroidery ring or frame.
◆ Transfer the design to the fabric.
◆ Embroider the piece, incorporating trapunto, applied textures and stitching.

PROJECT 12

◆ Prepare a design for a pattern applied in sections.
◆ Colourwash your fabric in a colour to suit the subject.
◆ Place the ground and fabric backing in an embroidery ring or frame.
◆ Transfer the design to the fabric.
◆ Embroider as you choose.

PRESENTATION

There are many different ways of presenting your finished piece of embroidery, the first being as a picture or wall hanging. Before you stretch the work you must decide whether or not it will look better mounted. There are three types of mount:

1) Plain cut card, the colour chosen to suit the work.
2) Fabric covered card.
3) Fabric covered padded card.

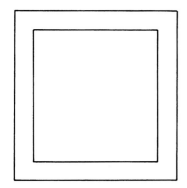

Card mount.

Sometimes a card mount can look quite harsh and to cover a mount with fabric adds a little softness to your picture.

Most framers will cut your mount for you and will even stretch your work to the necessary size. The best method of stretching, particularly if your embroidery is quite large, is to string the back up, then work from the centre outward.

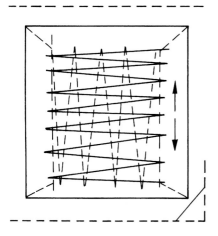

Stretching embroidery.

When stretching your work do not forget to allow extra material and the correct size of board for your mount. If your work is on the smaller side, say no larger than 35sq cm, you can make a very neat finish by using double-sided tape or adhesive. You must remember to turn the largest sides to the back first. The work is now ready to receive the mount and be framed up.

Mount 1

Plain cut card, the colour chosen to suit the work. The average border to allow all round your work is 5cm. An alternative is

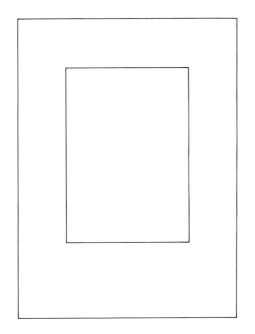

Alternative card mount.

to allow 5cm at the two sides and top and make the bottom larger by another 2.5cm for example.

Mount 2

Place your card mount to the reverse side of your fabric, allowing 2cm round all the

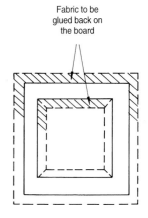

Fabric to be glued back on the board

Mount covered by fabric.

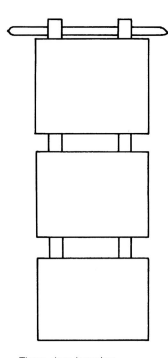

Three-drop hanging.

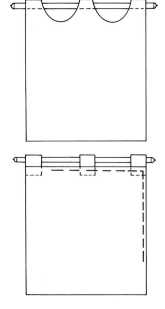

Different approaches to hangings.

sides for gluing back. Cut gently to the centre corners, using glue or double-sided tape. Bring back the centre fabric first, then attach the side pieces back on to the frame.

Mount 3

As mount 2, but first glue a light piece of wadding to the card, then cover the card with your fabric. This gives a much more professional finish.

If you prefer to place your work in a frame without a mount, there are many ready-made frames to choose from; your local framers should advise you on colour and size.

Another method of presenting your embroidery is to stretch your work, then attach it to the surface of a prepared board that has been covered with a complementary fabric. The embroidery is attached using double-sided tape to hold it firmly in position and a small curved needle to stitch all four corners down, leaving a border of at least 2.5cm.

Soft wallhangings

Your embroidery may require a softer presentation effect. You may therefore

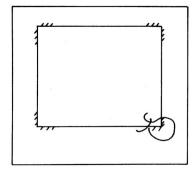

Fabric on a backboard.

choose to stretch it and attach loops so that it hangs softly from a rod; the work is attached to card, with the loops and tabs stitched to the back. Neaten the piece off and cover up all the ends of the loops by attaching a further piece of fabric to the whole of the back area. In this way you can hang one piece of work from another as illustrated in Chapter 4.

Another presentation method is to attach fabric at the rear of the piece, turning in all the edges, inserting loops at the top and hanging the work from a rod.

In general the overall colouring of your embroidery will dictate the colour of your mount and frame. If using rods these can be painted to suit your work. Nowadays, interior design changes with the seasons, and the choice of colours and finishes are numerous. Many framers will paint your frames in colours to suit your work, make the frame and mount look distressed, or use double mounts or box framing (generally used when your work has become very textured and 3D). It will pay you to look around at different framers to see what they have to offer and at what price.

Do remember that if your work is to be glazed the glass must never touch the work but should be raised by a fillet within the frame. So often I have seen textures flattened by the glass, spoiling the entire effect. Glazing is a matter of personal choice; I prefer not to use it, as I find that glass tends to remove a certain depth from the embroidery. It also alters the colour very slightly and the reflections in the glass are very distracting. I cannot stress enough how important the finish of your work is. Why embroider a beautiful piece of work and then use a mount which has been marked with glue or scratched, or even worse, a piece of glass with fingermarks on it? Make sure your work is neatly finished and the presentation is as good as your embroidery.

11 Advanced Techniques

By the time you have reached this stage of the book I hope you will have completed some of the projects set out. You should be equipped with a knowledge of the basic stitches and a few useful traditional techniques. I hope you have found it easy to follow and above all I hope you have enjoyed everything you have attempted.

Designing for embroidery was kept to a minimum for a very simple reason. When you paint paper or fabric you are dealing with a flat surface. When you start adding threads and textures you are dealing with a design that has weight, play of light, shadow and changes in colour tone. As you progress with your basic creative skills you will learn about design as you move from one piece of work to another. The ability to design will relate to your progression. Every craft is an ongoing learning situation, and it would be worthwhile visiting art galleries and embroidery exhibitions whenever you can. An interest in other crafts is also helpful, such as sculpture, wood carving and ceramics. All these lend inspiration in different ways.

There is no project work set out in the following chapters, however I hope that the illustrations and information will stimulate you into trying some of the different subjects covered. You must continue to be experimental in whatever you undertake, as this is very good for the imagination. Teachers can go on teaching you as long as you are prepared to learn and work, but at the end of the day it is your designs and embroidery that matter. Your own ideas and thoughts have a very important role to play as they will make your work individual and different. A good teacher will encourage you to try things for yourself, and not expect you to do everything he/she instructs.

Some examples illustrated in the following chapters were carried out by the more experienced students with very little help from myself. Some students are in the throes of learning, however, and require a little extra help to steer them in the right direction. As I have explained, learning is a continual process.

ADVANCED PURE EMBROIDERY

There are many different techniques that can be included in one piece of work. You could carry out pure embroidery stitches on a flat surface, or if your main concern is that the finished work should look as realistic as possible, think of all the different ways of creating it so. First and foremost, research your subject, obtain a good drawing or photocopy, include your own ideas regarding habitat, and apply some colour and notes on stitches and textures you wish to use.

The background fabric of the design at the beginning of the chapter is cotton, which has had a very pale colourwash. Painted on top with a very dry brush is

the suggestion of a pine tree. Part of a stump is shown, on which a bird rests. There is no fine detail in the painting at all, as this will come with the stitching. The head and upper wing of the bird have been padded by trapunto, which was firmly stuffed because the whole area was then covered in stitching. The chest and the front of the bird have also been covered with long and short stitch. The stitches can be small or large and can be made to resemble feathers or fur. I work with a single stranded cotton and sometimes two different colours in separate needles at the same time. You can achieve a good flow of stitches that look very lifelike.

The wing and tail feathers were made lifelike by using silk material. Firstly, fabric paint your silk, trace the feather shapes from your design, place the tracing on to your fabric and cut them out. If you cut these on the straight grain of the fabric, it will enable you to fray and cut giving a more realistic effect.

This is where experimentation plays such an important role in your work. You can of course apply straight and fly stitch to the top of the feathers, giving the suggestion of the quill and bars. The feet are very yellow so I chose to use gold leather cut to the shapes with some stitching on

Detail of head.

top. If necessary this could be padded as you stitch it down to give the effect of added weight.

You can clearly see that the beak is a piece of grey leather, padded as it is applied to the surface. Above the beak are nice crunchy French knots, and the eyes are in black patent leather. You really have to obtain a certain look with the eyes of a hawk, as the head is the focal point, and he must be clearly seen to be looking at you.

Note the impression given by the stump and pine branches; the stitching and depth of colour adds the necessary weight to the bottom of the picture, whilst the pine branches going right to the top right-hand side help to balance out the whole piece.

Once again, after researching the subject I drew up the cat, then I placed him into a habitat of foliage that gave me great scope for the use of textures. The head and nose were padded from the rear by

Detail of feathers.

Opposite:
The Hobby colourwashed and painted background (36cm x 23cm). Embroidered and applied with silk feathers

A servil (36cm x 33cm) with embroidered and applied foliage.

Sampler - painted, evenweave stitched with applied petals.

trapunto, the whole of the cat being worked in long and short stitch. Here again it was necessary to use several needles at the same time to obtain the shading. You will note that most of the stitches are quite long, proving that you can be quite brave with long and short stitch.

ADVANCED PAINTING

The following illustration is an impressionist painting taken from a birthday card. These paintings are ideal subjects to study for embroidery, as the strokes applied are merely colour marks, and it is their clever use that creates the picture. Monet's rivers and seas are full of mood; the cool of the day, quietness and solitude. All these thoughts can be portrayed in your work, not just in the design but in the clever use of gentle shading, the type of thread or the type of stitch you use.

Detail of the head. The nose, cheeks and brows have been stuffed from the rear.

The eyes are again the focal point, and must appear to be lifelike. I have created these from gold kid and black patent. The ears are also an important part of the animal as it must look as if it has just heard a noise. The foliage is a collection of straight stitch and French knots carried out in wool, whilst the leaves have been made on the sewing machine using several different fabrics, then attached to the piece to give a 3D effect.

The fabric has been colourwashed using fabric paint. Showing part of the sky brings light to the subject, whilst the field below is full of poppies, some fading in the hot sun. The poppies were painted on to the background using acrylics, applied with a rather dry brush. Further greens were applied to give deeper undergrowth and the necessary weight to the bottom of the design. Sweeps of barley

Poppy design colourwashed and painted with acrylics, stitched and quilted (46cm x 29cm).

were also added. The work was then complemented with simple embroidery and couched textured threads. One poppy has been covered with pale sheer chiffon to add to the effect of fading. The whole piece was then laid over wadding and quilted to add further depth.

The design shown at the beginning of the chapter started as a sampler of a painting on even weave linen, and again gives an impressionist effect. It is a very negative approach to painting, suggesting the flowers and the leaves. This painting was carried out using fabric paint, with a hairdryer at the ready in case the paint moved too quickly. The leaves were printed using real leaves, and some very simple stitches were applied to emphasize parts of the petals. Further petals and leaves were made by painting different silks and sheers then cutting them out and attaching them to the work. You could use iron-on vilene or singe the edges of these applied fabrics, as this will

stiffen them up and prevent them from fraying.

I then wanted to frame the piece, but without using an actual frame. I cut out strips of painted canvas and attached them to form a broken frame, adding variegated ribbon. I tried to imply that the flowers wanted to float about and didn't want to be imprisoned by a hard frame.

If you have been observant, you will have noticed that to paint a picture on fabric only requires enough embroidery to complement the whole painting. If you were to cover it completely with stitching, what was the point of painting it in the first place?

The *Dasies* design overleaf was adapted from a magazine picture. The cotton background was colourwashed as before, and the daisies painted in using acrylics applied with a dry brush. To achieve the effect of mist over the marsh, pieces of frayed sheer were laid over the watery areas. The entire piece was complemented

A detail of *Daisies*.

Daisies by Mary Hooper
(31cm x 33cm).

with simple embroidery stitches and some beads, and an added touch was made by attaching a machine-embroidered daisy.

Poetry in stitch is another aspect of embroidery that allows room to manoeuvre. Some students feel that they have to portray all of the verses, but if you read a poem through a few times, certain things will catch your imagination. You will find a starting point and sketch several ideas, then you can draw these individually and bring the best together to form a design that works for you. Your design may lend itself to a choice of finishes, such as a soft hanging from a rod, or even a triptych hanging, a simple picture or a cushion, or perhaps a 3D construction.

Poetry is a great source from which to draw for embroidery, and when I introduce this subject to a group of students, each person's impressions are very different.

'The Lady of Shalott'

On either side the river lie
Long fields of barley and of rye
That clothe the wold and meet the sky:
And thro' the field the road runs by
To many-tower'd Camelot;
And up and down the people go,
Gazing where the lilies blow
Round an island there below,
The island of Shalott.

Willows whiten, aspens quiver,
Little breezes dusk and shiver
Thro' the wave that runs forever
Flowing down to Camelot,
Four grey walls, and four grey towers,
Overlook a space of flowers
And the silent isle imbowers
The Lady of Shalott.

Tennyson

The *Lady of Shalott* by Gill Everest (47sq cm).

Gill composed this picture from research into figures and mythical castles, compiling the design to take in the willows and the river. She paints fabric in a very delicate way, and her needlework is just as fine. Gill takes great care with her work and it often takes her quite a time to complete, however I'm sure you will agree that it is time well spent. Her *Lady of Shalott* has been padded and carried out entirely in pure embroidery, giving a great feeling.

Note the flowing treatment of the hair and the delicate flower in her hand. The irises on the river bank and the fine embroidery depict the movement of the water.

Detail of The *Lady of Shalott.*

Detail of The *Lady of Shalott.*

The *Island of Shalott*, a 3D construction by Jean Bell-Currie (36cm x 20cm).

on to the fabric and let it run 'free', adding the vegetation in various greens, plus a hint of colour. Sometimes the colour ran too far or the petals showed the white fabric, however this lent itself to making the design lifelike and natural, and lovely pieces of work were accomplished. At the same time as the students painted the designs, they also applied paint to spare bits of silk, sheers, net and lace, to use in the same piece of work.

Hand embroidery was applied to complement the painting, and different fabrics were applied on the surface to form petals and foliage. The whole piece was then quilted to emphasize certain petals and leaves, adding extra depth and interest. The iris is a very noble flower and can look quite heavy, so enough fabric and work have to be carried out to the whole design to balance this.

Jean decided to create a complete 3D construction. She designed a tower which was then painted, setting it into an island and showing the flowing waters around it, giving her great scope for embroidery. A lot of thought had to go into the construction of the piece and Jean made a mock-up in stiff paper and card and worked out the mechanics of the subject first.

When you become a very proficient embroiderer you will probably set yourself added challenges to test your abilities.

Painting on silk

As I have said, silk painting is an entire subject on its own, and for this reason Jenny Milne, a silk painting tutor, was called upon to instruct my students on the different methods of applying vibrant colours to silk. All of the students were apprehensive at the thought of applying paint to such a wonderful fabric, but with clear guidance they set about it. Taking a flower of their choice, they lay the paint

Iris cushion by Joan Walters.

Wall hanging by Eileen Barden.

Blackberries by Pauline Lilley (21cm in diameter).

Eileen is relatively new to embroidery and was quite nervous of the challenge, but as you can see, she has created a very delicate hanging for a bedroom. Straight stitch, lazy-daisy and French knots and simple stitches were all that was needed. Petals sealed at the edges and a few leaves were added and the piece was then quilted. If you look closely, you will see a suggestion of painted petals; the flowers come to life through the added stitch and applied work.

Pauline is also new to this craft, but this piece, using a design of blackberries, was quite refreshing. Applied beads, French knots and simple stitches were all that was required. The work was then quilted and set into a round mount. Pauline always enjoys her work and overflows with enthusiasm, so much so that she has to be stopped before she adds too many beads and knots!

The grotto came about from playing with colour on silk, letting the colours flow together completely to cover the fabric. I then imagined what it could represent, and followed the change in the coloured lines with hand- and some machine-quilting, and applied net over one or two areas, trapping coloured beads. Hand stitching and couched threads were applied and some of the ends of the threads left to hang free. The piece of silk was then frayed all round and attached to a blue linen background, and the whole piece applied with couched wools and chenile to give continuous movement.

French knots and quilting
and beading.

Underwater by Ann Bickle.

whilst the sheer was frayed and anchored down at the same time. As the work progressed, couching, French knots and beads all played a part in creating the feeling of being beneath the sea. To maintain the effect of freedom, the cotton was frayed all round before being applied to a backboard covered in dark blue linen.

Although I try to encourage students to draw up their designs and map out a plan before commencing a project, it can be quite good fun to plan your work freely using a word as inspiration, in Ann's case 'underwater'. It forces you to think of that word and all it entails, and encourages you to use your imagination and experiment with your stitches and textures to see what you can achieve.

You can see how important it is to be flexible with stitch and texture, as it is only by being so that you can create movement and interest in the work. Most people like their paintings and embroidered pieces to resemble what they represent, and they do not necessarily want to carry out abstract work. A small number of people do carry out abstract pieces and enjoy their designs. I hope the design examples shown have proved how important it is to try your hand at painting your own fabrics; beginners have persevered and have been rewarded for doing so. We shall now move forward with colour and texture to more interesting subject matter for you to get your needles into.

This design was created from a piece of coloured silk, and would probably be considered slightly abstract.

This piece also grew as it progressed. *Underwater* was in Ann's mind when she applied the blue fabric paint to cotton for the background. At the same time colour was applied to small pieces of muslin and sheer. When all of these were dried and ironed, a selection of threads was chosen. The muslin was stitched on to the background forming rucks and channels,

ADVANCED SHADOW WORK

How often have you admired famous paintings of landscapes and skies? How often have you admired clouds laying across mountains and mists over meadows? A favourite photograph or postcard from your holidays would make a very good subject for the following type of shadow work. Today, embroiderers draw and paint the fabrics they work on, so why can't we draw a picture on paper then embroider on a sheer fabric, laying the embroidery over the drawing when finished? You can have one or two layers on top of the drawing, the latter being the most effective. This is still a form of shadow work, but expands the boundaries slightly.

Misty landscapes

STAGE 1

Mark out the size of the required picture on your drawing paper and allow an extra 5cm all round for a mount. Using a very soft pencil, for example '6B', very softly indicate the distant background, making sure the sky and hills occupy the top third of your design. Then, using the side of your lead, shade in the hills and background. It will take quite a time to achieve the sufficient depth of shading to show through your silk material, and you will need to lay the silk over your drawing from time to time until you have done this, but be very careful at this point because you do not want the lead to rub off on your fabric (pongee light silk is the sheerest).

STAGE 2

Having completed Stage 1 you must now start to add the middle distance, the trees and hedges perhaps. Include as much detail as possible, again making sure that it is showing through the material. To complete the drawing and increase the depth of tone, bring in your foreground. In this illustration this is the tree, rocks, stone wall and the suggestion of vegetation. Last of all lay your silk over the top, making sure you have sufficient depth in the overall design.

Some of the drawing will eventually be covered with embroidery applied to the silk, whilst some will show through, giving you a balance of drawing and embroidery. You must now seal your drawing by spraying it with a pencil fixative spray as this will prevent the lead from rubbing off on to the fabric. When you have reached this stage you may want to give thought to adding a light shading of blue pencil to the sky, and even a lake or pool if this is part of your design. If you prefer to leave it as it is, this will work equally well.

Having completed your design on paper, glue this to mounting card as you will now use this as a guide for your embroidery.

STAGE 1 EMBROIDERY

Working on an embroidery frame approximately the same size as your design, attach your silk to the frame using masking tape, getting it as tight as possible. Place the frame over your design and mark your four corners with a '1H' pencil. This is for guidance when holding your embroidery over your design and also acts as a guide when stretching your work over the card.

Holding your design under the silk you could now mark one or two places where you could commence your embroidery. Do not put any embroidery on the distant hills or you will spoil the whole effect. Your embroidery must be carried out in very fine threads, taking great care when you move from one place to another, as you will have to weave over your threads otherwise they will show through. Work your middle distance, or parts of it, first, leaving some of your drawing to show through. Work in very muted shades – grey, beige and perhaps a little soft blue and green.

You may wish to do a little more embroidery than shown here. When you are satisfied with the amount that you

First stage drawing for misty landscapes.

Second stage drawing for misty landscapes.

have done, remove the silk from the frame and attach it to your design card using glue. Attach the top and bottom first, making sure it is exactly in the marked places, then glue the sides.

STAGE 2 EMBROIDERY

You are now going to use a very fine sheer such as nylon chiffon or silk organza. Attach this to the same embroidery frame with masking tape and mark a few starting points with your '1H' pencil. Depending on your design, you may wish to introduce some different threads. On this layer you can get quite textual using couching, beads and French knots that will create interest in the foreground. You may want to add a little colour at this stage, applying a coloured sheer behind your chiffon or even on the surface. You could also leave the edges frayed to work in with your foliage. Slubbed threads couched down and thicker threads will help to give weight, feeling and perspective.

You will need to lay your work over the design all the time to ensure that the embroidery on the first layer shows through. Both layers of the embroidery are part and parcel of the finished design. When you have completed your embroi-

dery, mount this over your design completing the whole piece.

Because this work is very delicate, the colour of your mount and frame should complement the soft effect that you have achieved.

Many of my students have completed this subject, some finding it a little more difficult than others, but all have learned that the pencil is a very important part of the craft. Some students only complete one layer of embroidery in total, others complete the two layers in full. It has given the students a different approach to an old technique, although shadow work stitches such as herringbone have probably not been used; working on sheer and putting work beneath work has given the necessary shadowy effect. The different subjects covered by students include mountains, landscapes, fields of corn and poppies, and autumn and winter scenes, all in a range of colours.

Oak tree

Refer to your charcoal drawings of trees, as these shapes would be an ideal subject for shadow work. Attach your silk or chiffon to your embroidery frame with mask-

First stage of embroidery.

Completed embroidery.

ing tape. Mark a few places where you can start your work.

The trunk has been worked using various stitches together with the application of other bits of fabric. These were applied to the back, giving the old knurled effect. Beads and sequins are also used to give added weight and play of light. Some areas of foliage are shapes cut out from coloured sheers and placed on the back. Herringbone stitch is carried out on the surface as shadow work. You will see some of the sheers overlap, thus giving different tonal effects, and note that the colours of the threads are a little paler towards the top of the tree, giving it a lighter weighted appearance.

This tree has an autumnal feel, but there are many other ideas you could use; a spring or summer tree, even a crisp white winter tree. Think of words to describe your subject – a knurled oak tree, old and crusty with twisted roots, growths and knots; a shiny silver birch, smooth and slender, even regal. Thinking in this way helps you with your choice of stitches, techniques and fabrics.

Still life

Shadow work can be extended even further. In this example, the flowers are carried out in pure technique, and pieces of sheer and silk applied to the back, as shadow appliqué. The grapes also have silk and sheer applied to the back, and some have been stuffed with chopped wools. The apples are carried out in sheer, hand-made paper and trapunto. The whole piece is presented on a backing card that has been shaded with coloured pencils.

Designwise, this is a pleasing arrangement. The grapes and apples give weight to the bottom, whilst the eye travels upward to the lighter arrangement of flowers and leaves.

Soft furnishings and fashion

Shadow work has always been used in fashion, particularly for lingerie and bridalwear. In recent years it has been carried out by industrial machines. It is very fine and delicate by nature, yet has to withstand laundering, so carrying it out by hand has become very rare. The

Bodmin Moor by Jean James (36cm x 26cm).

only time this work, together with other embroidery, has been carried out by hand has been for extra special weddings and couture gowns, very beautiful, but very expensive. A friend of mine embroidered a veil for her daughter, and

Oak tree sampler (26cm x 34cm).

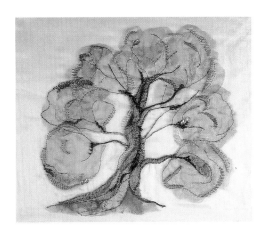

every woman in the family has since used it. It has been added to each time, with the initials and favourite flowers of each bride, and it is now a family heirloom.

When this technique is used for soft furnishings, it is slightly more limited. It can be used for sheer curtains that require decoration, or delicate cushions.

This cushion was purely an experimental piece of work. The design was taken from a drawing of a cyclamen, and was used to form a repeat pattern. The white satin was painted with fabric paints (I had my hairdryer at the ready just in case the paint started to run), sheer fabric laid over the whole piece, and hand embroidery added to complement it. The stems were then stitched by machine. This provided the channels for Italian quilting through which coloured threads were threaded. These threads were then threaded through to the surface to form tassels. The whole effect is very fresh and different.

Ideas

Choose a very rich colour as a base fabric, then work a design in pure shadow stitching on a much paler shade of sheer. These two fabrics can then be quilted together, the quilting making the fine stitching secure and durable.

Still life sampler.

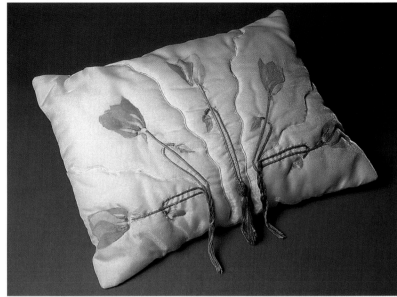

Painted and quilted cushion.

Design sheet of a
cyclamen.

12 Gardens

Gardens will always be a great source of inspiration for the embroiderer. Embroidery books exist on the subject of gardens alone, whilst you can also use photographs of your own garden or public gardens. Collect books on landscaping and garden designs, or cut ideas from magazine pictures that take your eye.

In this chapter we are going to explore different types of gardens, and the different ways of translating them into textiles. You may wish to base your design on your own garden, or use the suggestions above. Many of my students find it easy to plan a garden from their imagination, but bear in mind that to make it interesting you must have movement, texture and colour changes. Quiet and busy areas plus interesting corners should also be incorporated. The design is such that it takes the eye of the viewer into and through your garden. I encourage students to sketch their ideas on paper, as they may require a little help to achieve the correct balanced effect, or with the placing of the focal point. If you draw from the real thing, an interesting corner would be sufficient or two areas put together to form a design. It would also be a good idea to add colour using pencils and crayons, or to include plenty of notes and blocks of colour for reference.

Gardens can be approached from several different angles:

◆ As an architectural plan.
◆ Looking through the garden.
◆ A view through a gate, window, archway or door.

Always choose a view in which different shapes appear alongside each other, and which encompasses different textures, for example a shrubbery against a stone wall, a path leading to a summer house, a rockery as a backdrop to a pond. Focal points can include fountains, statues, urns and sundials.

Look for subtle changes in colour tone created by the different plant formations, which often overlay and encroach on one another. Make any notes that would be helpful when it comes to the embroidery, such as stitching suggestions, changes in colour, or shadows cast at a particular time of day.

As you can see this is a vast subject that excites the imagination, giving great scope for stitching and texture, and is well worth investigation.

Quick sketch in colour showing suggested threads and so on.

Opposite:
Canvas-work garden.

Calico garden by Dorothy Bennett (18cm x 13cm).

Calico garden by Margaret Halifax (18cm x 13cm).

CALICO GARDENS

This is one of the favourite subjects undertaken by students. Working in a single colour range is not just a learning discipline, it makes you think of one colour tone against another, coupled with the textures that you produce. This is where your imagination can run free.

Consider working with calico on calico and using only threads in the colour range – off-white through to soft beige and gold. Calico itself comes in different shades and weights, some nearly white, some quite creamy, whilst others can be naturally flecked. You may also like to refer to Chapter 9 for ideas.

Work on medium-weight calico for your background, also using a poly-cotton backing, framed up as tight as possible. Select your different threads in the colour range suggested, then design the garden on paper, indicating the overall size; 20cm × 12.5cm is an adequate size to complete. On your drawing indicate a path, bring it into your design and move

it through. Perhaps place a pond and a rockery to one side, and include a border, a lawn and maybe a tree.

This is where weight is very important, as if your embroidery is to be hung on the wall, you would need the main weight, and by this I mean the most embroidery, to be placed in the bottom two thirds of your design.

Start by working your path. Trapunto pebbles are very attractive, separated or even placed together. Use small pieces of card covered with calico or just plain satin stitch.

Indicate your pond by cutting a shape in sheer or net, or leaving the area as plain calico. You will be covering the edge with embroidery such as French knots, seeding or lazy-daisy, as all these stitches suggest soft creeping plant growth.

For the rockery, cut pieces of calico approximately 5cm × 5cm, carry out a close running stitch in a circle, carefully pull this up and stuff the shape so that the

Plan for a calico garden.

Calico garden by Sally Searle (24cm x 20cm).

result is nice and hard. Attach these in position. You can experiment with different fabrics for the stones, for example leather and suede, or even pieces of coloured tights over the calico. Also experiment with the sizes of the stones.

Leaf shapes can be embroidered before they are cut out. If these shapes are cut on the straight grain, each side of the leaf can be frayed back a little. Buttonhole bars can represent creeping formations, or can be carried out in circles to form flowers. Slubbed threads can be couched down in loops as a mass or moving around. This is where you must think of altering your colours and creating shadows.

You can keep the lawn area plain or seeding in some areas would be quite sufficient. If you would like a fruit tree in the lawn, fly- and creton stitch worked into a circle works very well, and using two shades of thread gives the tree more feeling; try using a thicker thread in a darker shade and a fine thread for a lighter shade.

Let us stay with this versatile fabric, calico, pushing the boundaries and looking at further ideas and its different applications.

Although Caroline has been a quilter for some years, she is new to creative

Garden through a gate by Caroline Nash (28cm x 23cm).

73

embroidery, and has a style all of her own. Her approach to the subject of calico gardens was quite different. 'I must have a gate, opening into a garden.' She has a passion for trees, so inside is a tree where she used plenty of very slubbed thread. There is a padded footpath, with embroidery and manipulation for growth.

The work was encased in a three-sided frame made from 2.5cm wood covered with calico. This was then covered with leaves made on the sewing machine and then cut out, plus further embroidery. You might think that the leaves are too big for the tree, however it actually works very well, casting deep shadows to the background. Caroline has expressed herself very well and really enjoyed the subject.

Detail of canvas-work garden.

CALICO AND OTHER TECHNIQUES

The design at the beginning of the chapter shows a calico padded mount complementing a piece of canvas work. When I did my training I was told that you never show the canvas unstitched, however today we can break all the rules, but only to achieve a good finished piece. The inner garden shows the canvas has been painted first, then simple stitches applied in colour to give a garden landscape finish. The calico embroidered mount lays on the surface and merges well with the background. The whole piece is presented on a backboard covered with calico.

This piece of work inspires different ideas – you could have a padded mount over a photograph, or a piece of black work but carried out in browns, or perhaps a small garden using one stitch only. Try out different ideas for yourself, but always remember that the embroidery on the padded mount must be an extension of the whole design. You will note that on

the illustration shown, the embroidery extends further on the left and overlays at the bottom and the right side, giving the entire piece good balance.

This detail indicates the steps from the mount going into the canvas work, and the French knots merging with the work behind. The colours used are also taken into account.

Tree cushion.

Calico is an ideal fabric for cushions. Here I have carried out a form of landscape by machine, but it could easily be done by hand. A distant ploughed field, hedges and trees bring you down to a river. The tree is worked on the surface by adding strips of calico and padding them out as they are stitched down, forming the trunk and the branches. Couched threads were then taken up and along the branches. The same threads hang free at the bottom to represent the roots. Wooden beads were then attached. The leaves were of a stylized shape, made on the machine, then attached by hand. The construction and the execution of the embroidery must allow for laundering; this cushion has been washed many times as it is favoured by our cat.

You can get quite carried away and do a complete 3D construction, as long as you spend some time thinking and planning, even making a mock-up in paper and card. This certainly helps in the construction, as you are able to work out any difficulties you encounter in advance.

First, I made the trunks using long lengths of firm wire threaded through calico rouleau. The wires were left exposed at one end for threading through to the base. I then made lots of separate leaves on the machine; some have a little fabric paint applied in a soft beige and terracotta colour. These were made with double fabric and a wire between and down the centres, the wires being long enough to be threaded down the trunk of the tree. The base was made as a separate unit on an embroidery ring. Many textures, rocks, pebbles, beads and stones were incorporated. The whole piece was then stretched over a hardboard base, and a hole was cut out of the centre so that the wires from the trunk of the tree could be threaded through and splayed out at angles to balance the tree. These wires were secured with a staple gun. The whole construction stands under a Victorian glass dome.

Calico gardens are a popular subject; beginners understand and finish beautiful work, whilst experienced embroiderers

The Farway Tree (23cm x 31cm).

Detail of *The Farway Tree.*

find it tantalising. It takes us from looking through a gate, to landscapes, soft furnishings, fashion and even 3D construction. When tackling the subject you will learn a lot about construction, as it is a problem solving situation at all times.

I myself was commissioned to make a replica of a vine room. All the windows were cut from card and covered with calico which was glued on the underside. The whole construction was then stitched together. Although most of the plant life was free machine embroidery on water soluble fabric the base sections were quilted with applied handwork and beads. I met many problems along the way, even though I had previously made a complete mock-up paper construction. You must persevere until you succeed.

You can see that I have worked on the same subject but turned it in many directions, from complete hand embroidery to total construction and free machine work.

COLOURED GARDEN THEMES

We can now move into the realm of colour, using different tones and looking into and through the garden. I have included a few suggestions for a title for your work:

◆ The seasons – winter, spring, summer or autumn.
◆ Colours – blue, green or red.
◆ Times of day – daybreak, evening time, sunset or moonlight.
◆ A cool garden, water garden, herb garden, bog garden, knot garden.

Choosing a title or theme such as these helps you in your choice of different coloured threads and materials and in the choice of colourwash to apply to your background.

The design

Refer to books, magazines, cards and photographs, or best of all draw from the real thing. Do not forget to adopt the eye of the viewer in your garden, moving through it up to the focal point such as a statue, obelisk or fountain. Roughly plan out your plants so that the heaviest are near the foreground and the formation of plant life becomes lighter in weight and colour further away. This will give the design weight towards the bottom thus creating the appropriate perspective.

Vine house by kind permission of Dr and Mrs DeGlanville (23cm long x 10cm wide, 18cm high).

Springtime by Jenny Ashley (46cm x 31cm).

Plan for a theme garden.

Fabric and threads

You can always work on purchased coloured background fabric and select your threads from your stock, but for this subject I would advise you to colourwash your background fabric and at the same time apply fabric paint to other bits of fabric you have in stock – lace, ribbons, white or cream threads, and any bits that you think will be useful to you in your design.

When colourwashing your background fabric, bear in mind the position of the focal point of your design, as it works well if that area is a shade lighter as this implies a shaft of light coming into the design.

Embroidery

Before you attach your background fabric and backing to your frame make sure you have sufficient material to allow for a mount. Some of you may wish to frame your finished work with a padded mount. In this case it is very important that you colourwash the mount fabric at the same time as the background. Having ironed all the colourwashed fabrics, frame up your materials ready for work. Decide how you are going to portray your focal point, using applied fabric, painted pelmet vilene, covered card or just trapunto. Complete this aspect first. Carry out your embroidery from the top of the design downwards, so that one plant formation lays on another in a realistic manner. Do not forget that the further away, the lighter in colour tone and less thick the thread, then as you work forward gradually mix your colours and the thickness of the threads until you reach the bottom of the work.

Here again, manipulation and textures come to the fore and will give weight and balance to your embroidery. Colouring all your fabrics and threads in shades of a single colour will give you a finished piece of work which is well blended.

This design of a garden and gazebo came from Jenny's imagination. The path gently moves through the garden up to

Detail of *Springtime.*

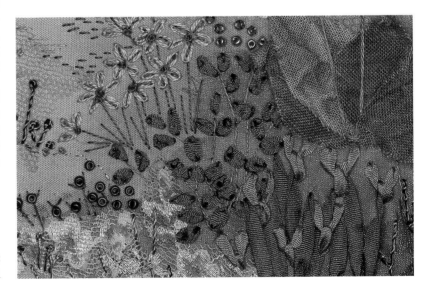

the focal point, and she has used a great variety of threads and other fabrics, all coloured at the same time. Lace has been used as well as large beads to form flowers, the clever use of manipulation with fine ribbons for flowers and French knots. What is particularly attractive is the green colour blending through to a green hinted with blue. This has been emphasized by the use of a varied textured thread.

This was a large panel that took a long time and a lot of work to complete, but was designed specifically for Jenny's lounge.

The padded mount in this illustration was painted to suit the three separate pieces of embroidery. The card mount was cut to receive the three panels, covered with wadding and then covered with the coloured fabric. It does take some time to achieve the correct finish for this type of mount, so that no puckering appears, particularly at the corners. It is very worthwhile, however, as it provides continuity between the three pieces.

There is a focal point in each piece, taking your eye up the stepping stones until you reach a resting place. You will notice the shaft of light appears to fall on the stepping stones, then travels upward, highlighted by a silver thread.

Desert Oasis by Joan Nunn (23cm x 28cm).

This design needed to convey a heated atmosphere. The colourwash background is lighter to one side, the light picking out the cobbles in the foreground very well. Coloured lace and beads provide further interest. Some of the foreground leaves have been cut from leather and machined, and fabric leaves cut out and applied. Here we have a box mount covered with silk in a darker shade which helps to give the piece distance. Note the irregular shape of the centre presentation.

With this subject there is again great freedom in the use of stitching and texture. Think of your title all the time when choosing the different techniques you wish to use, the soft subtle shadings and the gentle introduction of such things as ribbon, beads, shells or even covered washers. When thinking of your presentation you may consider the soft wall hangings that are quilted after the embroidery has been carried out. The hanging loops could be coloured to suit or a cord

Water Garden by Jean Bell-Currie.

Detail of *Water Garden.*

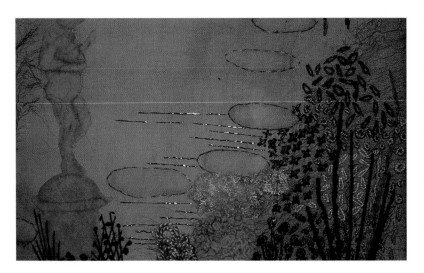

or tassels introduced. This would work particularly well if dealing with water as beads worked into tassels would echo the movement and play of light.

Thought could be given to perhaps a three-drop, incorporating morning, afternoon and evening, or a water garden through the times of day or seasons of the year.

I'm sure you have found this section on garden themes intriguing, and the illustrations a little different from the usual full-blown gardens in mixed colours. Using single colour tones you can create feelings of calmness and solitude through thought provoking words related to your chosen colour.

HERBACEOUS BORDERS

This is a different approach to the subject of gardens. Again you must plan your work first. Choose part of a garden that has plenty of depth; by this I mean full of growth and colour tones. When you take a photograph, take it from different angles and eye levels. Try looking through a border from a very low level – see how many different greens you can see. Are the different plants separated or intermingled? Because there are some very dark areas in a border, I choose to work over several different fabrics to achieve this effect. Make a sketch or plan for your design and add any notes and ideas on colour that come to mind. Two areas put together can form an interesting design. Please note that working entirely from a photograph can give a rather flat appearance to the embroidery, and photographs are better used to recall colours and detail. There is nothing to replace your own ideas and feelings at the time of sketching to create an original piece of work.

Green materials of all kinds are one of the best props you can have. When you become an avid embroiderer you will collect all manner of things – wool, beads, washers, balsa wood, lollipop sticks and wires to name but a few. These do not sound like embroidery tools but you will be surprised how such things become a must.

Plan of fabrics and suggested threads.

Spring Harmony (13cm x 18cm).

Summertime (13cm x 18cm).

Bondaweb. This will give you a different coloured background on which to apply your needlework. If you intend to introduce some trapunto you would need a poly-cotton backing on your working fabric. Put your prepared fabric on your frame or ring and commence your embroidery from the top, working downwards. This creates the deeper effect of colours showing through because you will be embroidering plant formations one on top of another.

Spring Harmony

The sky was coloured using a blue pencil, green fabrics and mohair worked over with straight- and creton stitch, lazy-daisy and couching, twisted buttonhole bars and loopy French knots, variegated threads and stranded cottons. The path is formed from small pieces of leather in the foreground, turned over to the suede side to imply distance. Fabric leaves have been cut out and sewn in to achieve a 3D look. You will note that the work is heavier in the bottom third, giving it perspective.

This sampler was inspired by a magazine picture. The background is fabric painted poly-cotton with a small piece of coloured sheer. Most of the work is in French knots, some very neat and fine, others quite loopy. The foreground is painted felt, with straight stitch, some machine work and bullion knots. Using the felt was an experiment to try and achieve the depth of the foreground.

Because you are creating a dense undergrowth effect and working in many colours, these pieces of embroidery are better presented in a very simple way; a natural wood frame is quite sufficient.

Refer to your sketch or design source and select small pieces from your green fabrics to fit certain areas. These could perhaps be frayed a little at the edges then applied in position on your ground fabric. Fix them by using bonding powder or

Summertime

Composed from creton-, fly- and straight stitch, lazy-daisy and French knots, stranded cottons and some variegated perle, chopped ribbon and applied leaves. A patterned fabric has been experimented with for the pathway. All the colours used are to portray a warm summer's day.

13 Design Sources

Once you have gained experience with different techniques you will want to stretch yourself further and will need to try something with more depth, to test your design ability. There are many tantalising fabrics and other mediums we can turn to, such as metal, foil and thread, or burned and distressed fabric. Experimentation can lead to some very interesting mixed media work.

I would suggest that you choose one subject to study. Research it well using the library, photocopying designs, collecting pictures and fabrics and so on. Take time to do this as it can be just as pleasurable as the needlework itself. Overlay one design on to another and play with the shapes and colours and you may get a few surprises. Ideas may flood your head and you may need to do some small samplers using different techniques. Do them quite quickly as often spontaneous ideas work quite well. You may even find you will come up with a design that is not wholly related to the subject you started with.

IDEAS

Poetry

I have already mentioned this in Chapter 11. Nature poems are particularly good to translate into embroidery, whilst children's books of poems are also full of ideas.

New materials and threads: metal and varied threads, sheet fibres for heating, metal foils and material.

Opposite:
Clinoclase by Jean Bell-Currie (38cm x 49cm).

Music

This could be quite a challenge, particularly classical music, whilst popular music could lead on to various different subjects. Take *The Blue Danube* for example. What comes to mind? List all your thoughts – a waltz, a river, water in all its forms, swirling, gliding smoothly. My mind then turns these words into shades of silver blues, sea greens and crystal pools. There are many songs that conjure up colour and atmosphere – *Greensleeves*, *Sing a Rainbow* and *An English Country Garden*.

Minerals

From a book on minerals and gems, various large and small photocopies were laid before a class, and most students worked straight from these pictures, whilst others were inspired by various fabrics. The crystal formations and jagged edges were interpreted using painted balsa wood, thick pelmet vilene, wrapped matches and covered lollipop sticks. Some of the pieces were quite complicated, some pure embroidery, but all were interesting and worked very well. The following illustrations show the different approaches given to the crystal 'clinoclase'.

The background fabric of the design at the beginning of the chapter was colourwashed to suit the subject. Some areas were padded and other fabrics applied. Small circles were pleated, some were frayed. Molten lead shapes were added, and currons (buttonhole circles, the bottonhole being worked over a thread taken around a small cylindrical object such as a pencil) were applied, stitched down and hung free to add movement. The entire piece was then presented on a backboard covered with painted silk paper.

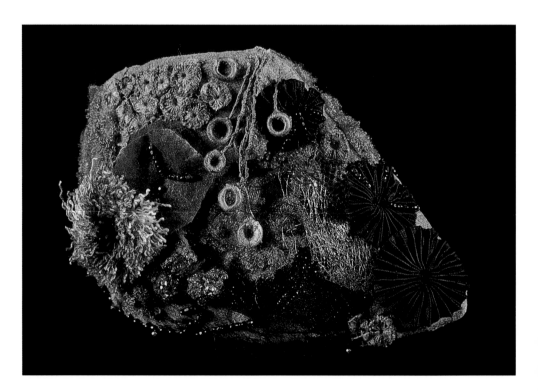

Clinoclase stone by Jean Bell-Currie.

By this stage Jean had gone into over-drive, arriving at class having covered a real smooth stone to match her hanging. It can be so nice to get carried away by a new subject.

Vera's clinoclase is pure embroidery – a very subtle colourwashed background, padded areas, applied fine fabrics and manipulated silk, couched variegated ribbon, threads and pure embroidery stitches. As you can see the embroidery was expertly carried out. It is the clever use of colours and the flowing application that pulls the piece together and gives a great sense of freedom.

Landscapes

Many people are fascinated by different types of landscape – rolling hills, moor-land, forestry, mountains and lakes. You may find it quite inspiring to prepare a paper collage first.

Collect coloured papers from maga-zines, or paint your own using acrylic or Brusho paints, giving different effects by stippling or sponging one colour on to another. Tear paper shapes and place them over each other, creating your land-scape. You can then transfer this into fabrics, fraying the edges, and even intro-

Clinoclase by Vera Whitting.

Painted paper landscape.

or all three types of quilting; lay pieces of different coloured fabrics over each other, stitch your design then cut back to the required colour (this can be very vibrant).

Natural phenomena

This subject can result in some very colourful and exciting designs – fire, lightning, ice, snow, earthquakes, volcanoes and whirlwinds. Carry out your research into the subject, bringing together all your ideas and thoughts. Take fire, for example, different reds and oranges, glowing intense colours, sparkling, smoking, flashing and moving. This is where you can use exciting and vibrant materials such as beads and metal threads, manipulation, cutting back, fraying and slashing.

Some of these ideas could result in an abstract design, but nevertheless they are very thought provoking. You will become far more adaptable to different ideas, which will make you more versatile when faced with unusual subjects.

ducing some hand-made paper, nets and sheers. Apply padding if required; the stitching and textures will bring the whole piece to life. Do not forget that landscapes alter with the changing light of the day and the seasons.

Pattern

This is found everywhere you look – architecture, insects, feathers, flowers, vegetation and general man-made objects. Taking leaves as an example, arrange them in different ways, back to back, overlapping, large on small and so on. This type of design can be utilized in many ways, from a hanging to a jacket or cushion. Think of the different ways that you can turn your design into textiles – painted then embroidered; quilted in one

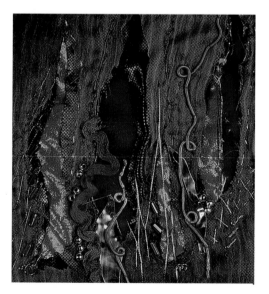

Fire sampler.

14 Free Machine Embroidery

So far we have covered embroidery from basic stitching through to the creative use of fabric and threads. Free machine embroidery is as creative as you can get, because you not only draw with the needle but you can make up your own fabrics using a base of water soluble material.

If you have a machine and it is equipped with the ability to drop the feed teeth or with a cover plate supplied, then it is quite possible that you can acquire the skill of free machine embroidery. There are now three forms of machine embroidery:

1. Stitching patterns using the set stitches within the machine.
2. Drawing freely with the machine needle.
3. Computerized designing.

We shall deal only with free machine embroidery. This is a technique where you draw with the needle, creating your own designs and applying many fabrics. It is a very exciting form of embroidery and one that you can get totally hooked on. Those of you who are about to try this for the first time, follow the instructions one step at a time.

◆ Clean out your shuttle casing.
◆ Oil your machine (modern machines may not require this).
◆ Before altering your machine, thread it up and run the machine on running stitch to check the tension.

◆ Insert a new needle (different machines have different needles), size 80 (11) or 90 (14).

If running correctly you are now ready to reset for free working.

◆ Thread up with different coloured cottons on the top and in the shuttle.
◆ Set your machine stitch to '0'.
◆ Drop the feed teeth or cover with a plate (see the instruction book).
◆ Frame up calico or cotton into a clasp embroidery ring (a small wooden ring can also be used).
◆ Take off the foot and replace with the darning foot. (If the darning foot is not supplied, sew with the needle only.)
◆ Lower your pressure foot.
◆ Roll your needle by hand to bring your shuttle cotton to the top.
◆ Place the ring under the needle ensuring that the material is flat to the bed of the machine. Roll your needle into your fabric before applying the power.
◆ Apply a medium speed and start to draw.

It is most important that you move your ring very slowly and smoothly. Medium power must be applied; if the speed is too slow you could miss stitches. Because the feed teeth are dropped you are in complete control of the machine. Try to fill your material in a controlled way, creating circles and lines and letting the stitches build up until you feel quite relaxed with the process. Alter your

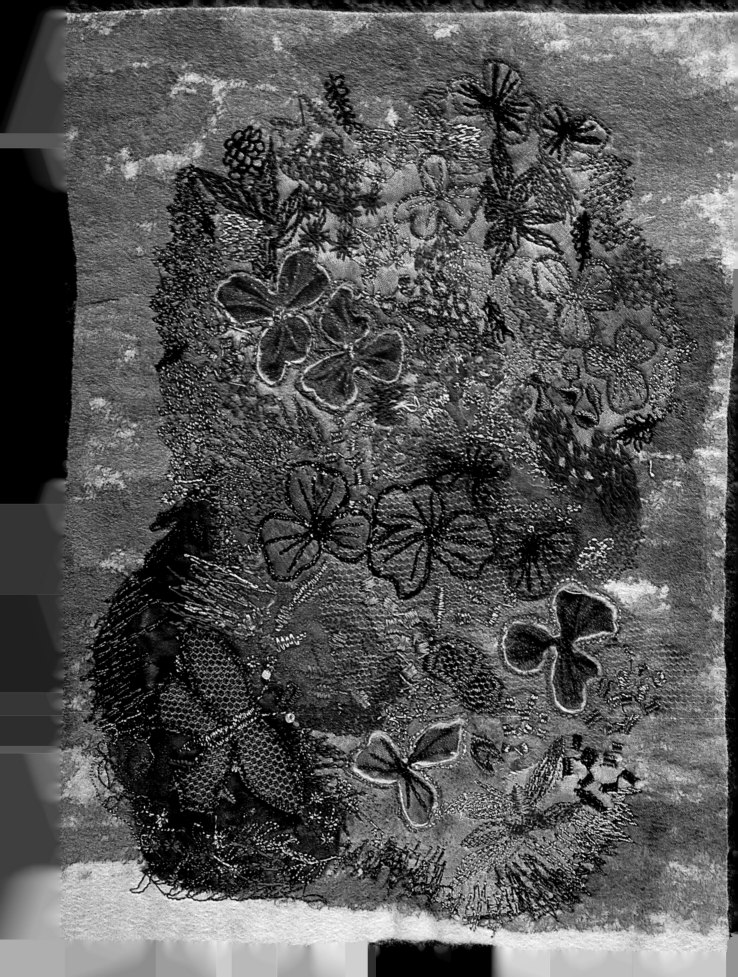

movements up and down and side to side. You will find that you can move the ring in any direction. It will take a lot of practice, but when you can achieve it there is such a lot more you will be able to accomplish with your creative work.

If the cotton breaks you could be moving your ring too quickly or the top tension might require slackening a little. If you are getting a lot of mess piling up at the back of the work you will probably find that your pressure arm has not been lowered (this is often the case with a beginner).

When you have mastered running stitch, thread up your machine with colours for leaves, draw different shapes on your fabric with a marker pen and embroider. Make two running stitched lines all round the shapes, as this will enable you to cut them out easily to use on your embroidery. The same process is carried out for flowers, and you could of course use coloured fabrics.

You can become quite inventive, using different fabrics on top of each other, net

Beginner's work – leaves and flowers.

Beginner's machine work.

Opposite:
Free work on painted felt by Janet Legg.

on cotton, sheer on silk, or any combination that results in the colour and texture required. Experiment from your stocks, save all your sample work, and make any necessary notes that come to mind for your reference. You will see from these samples that this type of embroidery can lead you to 3D application such as decoration for bags, hats and pockets. You can create soft natural hangings, or apply the technique to quilting and soft furnishings.

We can now move on to zig-zag. Set your machine to a medium width of stitch. Take great care to move your ring very slowly, building up your stitches as you go. Because you are using the width of the slot in the plate for your stitches, the movement of the ring is paramount, as too quick a move can break your needle.

This piece of work shows fabrics applied over cold water soluble material called aquafilm, building up a collection of leaves and flowers throughout the work. Hilary only used running stitch during the design. When working on this material, you must remember to join up and overlap in a very firm way. If you do not, it could fall apart when wet. (Using soluble fabric is an aquired skill, but the fabric is being improved all the time, and is becoming quite strong.)

Janet decorated a piece of felt that had previously been painted. Apart from drawing freely which she clearly enjoyed, she has applied coloured sheer to the back of the felt, cutting away the surface felt to reveal coloured flowers. She has also played about with some set stitches, using them in a block form and moving them around. There is great scope here for further experimentation.

Work carried out on cold water soluble fabric by Hillary Jepp.

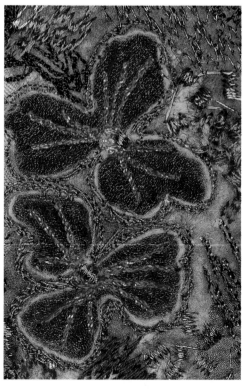

Free work on felt by Janet Legg.

Even if your machine is an old one do have a try, just coming to terms with the running stitch and the zig-zag can be quite fascinating. There are many more technical things you can achieve by altering tensions on the machine and the shuttle, but I would recommend you obtain a book on the subject or perhaps attend a class or two; a hands-on session with a tutor is often all you need to set you on the right track. Some people regard machine embroidery as cheating, but it is simply a completely different approach and is certainly a form of embroidery. Drawing with the needle, using many fabrics and building up surfaces of your own can lead to some very interesting results. With the new computerized machines, you can draw your own designs, scan them and the machine will do the rest.

My own machine is a standard Bernina and is now fifteen years old. I regard it as my very best friend, and it has travelled miles in the course of teaching.

When visiting exhibitions you will see that the percentage of machine work is increasing. It is hoped that this work will run alongside the beautiful hand embroidery carried out today.

The work opposite was done completely by machine. The water is dyed silk chiffon, the trees either side are made up of strips of different hessians and added cords, and chopped up fabrics, machining one piece over another until the correct depth of foliage is obtained. The distance at the top is achieved using cold water soluble fabric, whilst the foreground is a combination of applied fabrics, some of which are dyed and painted. The stones in the water are created using hand-made paper applied at the back and on the top.

The Deep is based on deep sea colours, the movement of waves and swirling water. It was a piece of work which evolved from much experimentation with colouring silk and sheers, and

the working of many small samples. The finished work is in three sections – a backing of thick textured hand-made paper, a machine-embroidered and quilted piece with areas completely cut out revealing the hand-made paper, and a final piece of sheer and felt machined and wired. The surface had covered beaded

Polson Bridge, the old entrance to Cornwall (65cm x 44cm).

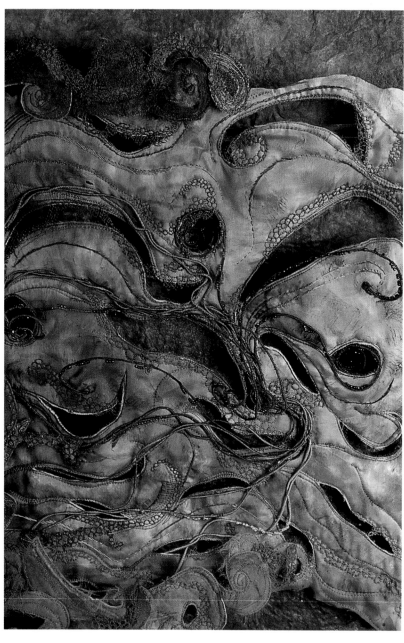

The Deep (36cm x 50cm).

wires added to form wave shapes and swirling pools and the whole piece is mounted on clear perspex.

Most of my work is a translation of what I see and feel, how and what I use is where the interpretation takes place. Because we are encouraged to experiment, we can often produce something that is unusual, yet still portrays one's feelings and thoughts on the chosen subject. This chapter gives only a small taste of free machine embroidery; it gives us the freedom to work in 3D and to complement our handwork, and takes us into the realm of interesting fabrics and effects. It is a technique that does take practice but is extremely worthwhile.

Conclusion

Having achieved some traditional techniques and explored the more creative side of embroidery, you will no doubt want to learn more and progress with your design and experimentation. Because a wider range of materials is becoming available it is always good to ask questions:

◆ Are some of these commodities promoting embroidery to move forward?

◆ Are they all durable and long-lasting?
◆ Is the finished work contrived or well thought out and executed?

Try not to be influenced too greatly by other embroiderers' work; follow your own thoughts and explore them, as these are the best stepping stones to individual expression. The future is an expanse for us to fill with exciting ideas.

Suppliers

Whaleys (Bradford Ltd)
Harris Court
Great Horton
Bradford
West Yorkshire
BD7 4EG

A full range of ready-to-dye fabrics including silk, felt and water soluble.

Borovicks Fabrics Ltd
16 Berwick Street
London
W1V 4HP

Exotic fabrics and sheers.

DMC Creative World
Pullman Road
Wigston
Leicester
LE8 2DY

DMC threads.

Silken Strands
20 Y Rhos
Bangor
North Wales
LL57 2LT

Machine- and hand-embroidery threads. Solubles, Bondaweb and beads.

Leila Sutcliffe
21 Hitch Lowes
Chelford
Cheshire
SK11 9SR

A wide selection of hand dyed threads.

Madeira Threads UK Ltd
Thirsk Industrial Park
York Road
Thirsk
North Yorkshire
YO7 3BX

Machine- and hand-embriodery threads.

EMBROIDERER'S GUILD

UK
UK Embroiderer's Guild
Apartment 41
Hampton Court Palace
East Molesey
Surrey
KT6 9AU

USA
The Embroiderer's Guild of America
200 Fourth Avenue
Louisville
Kentucky
40202
USA

Australia
The Embroiderer's Guild of Australia
175 Elizabeth Street
Sydney
NSW 2000
Australia

New Zealand
Association of New Zealand Embroiderer's Guild
171 The Ridgeway
Mornington
Wellington 2
New Zealand

Canada
The Canadian Embroiderer's Guild
PO Box 541
Station B
London
Ontario
N6A 4W1
Canada

Index

Other Titles in the *Art of Crafts* Series